SPANISH NOTEBOOKS

BOOKS BY IVAN MAISKY

Before the Storm
Journey into the Past
Who Helped Hitler?

TRANSLATED BY RUTH KISCH

*Studies in the Agrarian History of England in
the Thirteenth Century*
by Academician E. A. Kosminsky (Basil Blackwell, 1956)

IVAN MAISKY

SOVIET AMBASSADOR TO THE UNITED KINGDOM, 1932–43

MEMBER OF THE ACADEMY OF SCIENCES OF THE U.S.S.R.

Spanish Notebooks

TRANSLATED FROM THE RUSSIAN BY

RUTH KISCH

HUTCHINSON OF LONDON

HUTCHINSON & CO (*Publishers*) LTD
178–202 Great Portland Street, London W1

London Melbourne Sydney
Auckland Bombay Toronto
Johannesburg New York

★

First published in Russia as
ISPANSKIYE TETRADI
(Voyennoye Izdatelstvo Ministerstva Oborony SSSR 1962)

English edition: first published 1966

Dedicated
to those who fought for the Spanish Republic

CONTENTS

IN PLACE OF PREFACE

A QUARTER of a century has passed since the time when the Spanish Fascists, led by General Franco, and encouraged in every possible way by Hitler and Mussolini, began a revolt against the government of the Spanish Republic. That quarter-century has been filled with immense events, events of historic significance for the whole world. Yet progressive humanity to this day retains undimmed the memory of close on three years of war fought by Spanish democrats against Fascism and its patrons, open and concealed. There are two main reasons for this.

First, the war of 1936–9 in the Iberian peninsula contributed a shining and unforgettable page to the history of democracy the world over, not only in Spain. It was a war of the forces of progress against the forces of reaction, of the forces of peace against the forces of war—one of the most just of wars.

Secondly, the war of 1936–9 in the Iberian peninsula—and this becomes especially clear in the light of history—was a battle of the advance guard in the second world war. It was not just a civil war between two camps within Spain itself. It was a civil war plus very powerful, very active foreign intervention, in which the major powers of Europe took part, as did the U.S.A. This came out especially clearly in the activities of the so-called 'Committee for Non-Intervention in the Affairs of Spain', which came into being in London in September 1936.

Now, at this present time, when Latin America is rising up in its great struggle for liberation from the chains of U.S. imperialism, it is helpful to recall the experience gained in the heroic struggle of the Spanish democrats a quarter of a century ago. It is likewise extremely important to visualise clearly the international setting in which the Spanish war of 1936–9 took place, the balance of forces in the world arena as a result of which the fall of the Spanish Republic became possible. What will be related in the following pages is of the most direct relevance to precisely this international aspect of the Spanish war.

During the years of the war it was my lot to work as Soviet Ambassador in London, and to represent the U.S.S.R. on the Committee for 'Non-Intervention'. I want to show here what went on inside the Committee, and the nature of the historical situation in which it functioned.

My frank narration of the events of those days will serve, I think, to expose many reactionary legends brought into being by bourgeois politicians, historians and journalists.

IVAN MAISKY

Translator's Note

THE full text or stenographic record of the Proceedings of the London Committee for Non-intervention in Spanish Affairs has never been made available to the public. In the present work Mr. Maisky supports his interpretation of the tenor of the Committee's deliberations and actions by forceful quotations from the actual speeches and contributions to discussion made at its meetings. These quotations are fully authenticated, the Foreign Office having given permission for the documents to be consulted in their library; the remarks made by various parties therefore appear as originally uttered and recorded, not re-translated from the Russian. Unless there is a footnote to the contrary, it should be assumed that all passages in quotations are taken from the stenographic notes at the Foreign Office Library which are available for inspection.

RUTH KISCH

I

First alarms

On 11 July 1936 Alvarez del Vayo came to see me. He and Largo Caballero were in London for the Seventh Congress of the Amsterdam (Trade Union) International, and he did not want to return to Spain without seeing the Soviet Ambassador to Britain.

We sat and drank tea in the Embassy conservatory. I was considering my visitor with close attention. Alvarez del Vayo was known to me by name. I knew he was a left-wing Spanish socialist and a well-known political journalist, and that in the early years of the Republic, under the Left Republican Azaña government, he had been Ambassador to Mexico, and then had been appointed to the same post in Moscow. But the reactionaries who came to power at the end of 1933 had cancelled his appointment; and Alvarez del Vayo remained a member of parliament only, and as such carried on a determined fight against all attempts to restore the semi-feudal monarchy. I was now seeing Alvarez del Vayo for the first time, and my interest was entirely natural.

Long diplomatic practice had trained my memory to act as a sort of photographic plate, which would without difficulty take up all the characteristics of the people I met. Their appearance, words, gestures and intonations were rapidly recorded on this plate, building up into sharply defined, detailed images. Often I would reach a mental conclusion about a person—positive or negative, with or without qualifications—on the spot, straight after our first acquaintance.

My conclusion on Alvarez del Vayo on that far-off July day was positive, but with one qualification . . . that will come later, though.

Of course, our talk revolved all the time around political questions. Alvarez del Vayo cross-questioned me in detail on the European situation, on British policy, on Soviet views on international affairs. I did my best to satisfy his enquiries, so far as I could and might do so, and in my turn cross-questioned him on the situation in Spain.

On 16 February 1936 fresh elections to the Cortes had taken place. They gave a great victory to the parties of the Left. But the forces of reaction did not propose to abandon their age-old positions. A fierce struggle was in progress throughout the country between Left and Right, a struggle the external manifestations of which were not always easy for us, spectators on the side-lines, to understand. It was especially difficult to form any clear idea of what direction Spain was moving in—towards a stronger democratic republic or towards the triumph of semi-feudal monarchist dictatorship? So I naturally availed myself of the opportunity to get as full and precise a picture as possible from my guest. Alvarez del Vayo readily answered all my questions.

In the course of the conversation I remarked in passing: 'I can well believe that the broad masses of the Spanish people are in radical or even revolutionary mood. I can believe that there are anti-feudal and anti-clerical feelings among the intellectuals, among various small groupings within the bourgeoisie, even among a few of the landowners. But in whose hands is the army? A great deal can depend on that, as things develop further.'

Alvarez del Vayo finished drinking his tea, set his cup down on the table, and after what seemed a pause to gather his thoughts together began: 'I find it hard to answer that briefly. May I explain in a little more detail the situation regarding the armed forces in Spain . . . ?'

I readily agreed, and Alvarez del Vayo told me this:

On 14 April 1931, when Spain was proclaimed a Republic, the

army represented a grave problem for the new government. The main mass of Spanish army officers had always been recruited from semi-feudal landowning circles and was remarkable for its extremely reactionary outlook. The numbers of high-ranking officers were astoundingly high. In that same year, 1931, there were about 200 generals and 17,000 officers for an army numbering 105,000 on active service, or 1 general per 500 soldiers and 1 officer per every 6 other ranks. A patently ridiculous ratio, bearing in mind the very low level of technical equipment of the Spanish army in those days. And there were thousands more officers and generals in the reserve! Military expenditure accounted for almost one-third of the total state budget.

The army (or rather its upper crust of generals and officers), that trusty shield of Church and landowner, was a real state within the state, and at its head was the king himself. There was not the slightest doubt that if the Republic wanted to put its own life out of danger it must immediately destroy so dangerous a wasps' nest.

Had the Republic done so? Only partially, half-heartedly.

The first Republican Minister for War, Azaña, had tried to 'reorganise' the army, but, like a typical liberal democrat, he was unable in doing so to act sufficiently firmly or consistently. Instead of completely breaking up the old upper echelons of the army and creating new ones, of men well disposed towards the Republic, Azaña chose the path of unsound compromise. He proposed that all officers who did not hold republican views should go into voluntary retirement, retaining their full pensions, arms, uniforms and titles of rank. In this way the numerical strength of the corps of officers was approximately halved. But politically speaking little was changed. The officers who remained in the service changed their outward tinge slightly, but inwardly preserved their former monarchistic and feudalistic convictions. And those who went on to the reserve, finding themselves entirely free from their usual duties, dived head first into 'political work'; they created the 'Spanish Military Union' (*'Union Militar Española'*), which later became a bulwark of reaction, they established close contact with the extreme right-wing parties and groups, they started organising military conspiracies and rebellions. And all at public expense! The Republic conscientiously paid out their pensions.

Alongside the army there was in Spain a large gendarmerie also, known as the *Guardia Civil*. It had the worst possible reputation among the masses of the people. It was equally well hated by the workers and the peasants. At the time of the 1931 change of power the *Guardia Civil*, under General Sanjurjo, did not dare to come out openly against the Republic: the Bourbons were too badly discredited just then! Besides, Sanjurjo considered that the French *'plus ça change, plus ça reste'* was fully valid for Spain. But he was wrong. Spineless though Azaña and his colleagues might be, they nevertheless found themselves obliged, under pressure from the awakened masses, to begin certain reforms, in particular land reform. This provoked a storm of resentment among the Spanish reactionaries. The generals reacted promptly: in August 1922 Sanjurjo, relying on the support of the *Guardia Civil*, raised a revolt against the government. It was ill prepared and mainly confined to Seville. The main forces of the ruling class were biding their time; they felt military action was premature. The workers for their part responded to the revolt by a general strike.

Sanjurjo's rash adventure was mopped up within a few hours. It might, however, have served as a serious warning to the government.

Azaña was presented with an excellent opportunity to disband the *Guardia Civil* completely and to create in its place a new police force loyal to the Republic. But no! Even now Azaña did not change his unsound, compromising tactics: after being condemned to death Sanjurjo was pardoned, the Guardia Civil was preserved in its old form, while at the same time the government brought into being a special Assault Guard (*Guardias de Asalto*) recruited from supporters of the new régime. In this way Spain found herself possessed of two security bodies which were far from seeing eye to eye with one another on all issues—a situation which gave rise to extremely dangerous administrative chaos in the country.

Alvarez del Vayo frankly admitted that the harmful effects of this policy had made themselves felt with especial force after the elections in February 1936, in which the Popular Front gained a majority in the Cortes. The Spanish reactionaries were really frightened, and, having no confidence in their ability to avert the threat to their economic and political privileges by parliamentary means, began to think seriously of the gambit so frequently resorted to in Spain—a military *coup* or *'pronunciamento'*. The political importance of the army and the gendarmerie was at once increased.

Did the Republic take any steps to defend itself? Yes, it did. Alvarez del Vayo informed me that 'the most suspect' of the generals had been sent away as far as possible from Madrid, that a purge of the officer corps was being made, that the Assault Guard was being strengthened. Further, the socialist youth league had created its own militia. On summing up all this, comparing the debit and credit items, Alvarez del Vayo came to this somewhat optimistic conclusion: 'Of course, the path of the Republic is not strewn with roses, but it is not in serious danger. There are forces in the country sufficient to avert or in any event crush any attempt at a military *coup*.'

Having heard Alvarez del Vayo out, I remarked that his story left me with a rather different impression: 'After all, consider what this position amounts to. The Assault Guard is cancelled out by the Civil Guard. The army is extremely unreliable, for in spite of all Azaña's reforms the main mass of officers remains very reactionary. Sending "suspect" generals away to the provinces can really hardly be considered a serious preventive measure. So in practice the army is in the hands of the enemies of the people. And what can the democrats set against it? Only the socialist militia . . . How large is it?'

'In Madrid it numbers up to 15,000 or so, I think,' answered Alvarez del Vayo.

'And how well trained and armed is it?'

'Not at all badly trained, I should say. . . . Especially if you have morale in mind. But as to arms, things are not too good. . . .'

'There you are, you see,' I went on. 'Against a large and well-equipped army you have a small and badly armed socialist militia. Of course the morale of the militia is a very important factor in your favour, but——'

'But the people is with us!' exclaimed Alvarez del Vayo, 'the broadest masses of the people!'

'That is very important, of course,' I agreed, 'that is the main strength of the Republic. But if the people wants to defend its rights to any purpose it must have sharp teeth. So far as I can judge, the Spanish people has not got such teeth yet. And that is very dangerous. The forces of reaction can easily decide to gamble on a *coup*, all the more easily since a *pronunciamento* is practically an everyday occurrence in your country. . . . One must not forget the international situation either, the plans and ambitions of the Fascist powers, Germany and Italy . . .'

Alvarez del Vayo started to object. He was determined not to give up his optimism, which appeared less and less justified to me the longer we argued. In the end I said to him: 'I hope with all my heart that your expectations will be realised. But for myself I regret to say that I feel sceptical. I think that the danger to the Republic is very real. If the Republic does not succeed in "cleaning up" the army thoroughly, and in the shortest possible time, and in taking a firm hold upon it, one can be sure of nothing. To gain real control of the army and to arm the people —that is the most important task for democracy in Spain, and for the Socialist Party in particular.'

'That is what we are doing!' Alvarez del Vayo responded with warmth. 'But what we can do is strictly limited. We Socialists are not in the government, you see, we are only in support of it. The government is made up of people like Azaña. All that can be done under conditions as they are at present we are doing, and will go on doing. Have no doubts on that score. . . .'

When Alvarez del Vayo had gone I began to draw up a mental

balance-sheet of our conversation. It was quite clear to me that there was something too trusting about my departed guest, too soulful almost. And alas! I knew too well that the rose-tinted spectacles of even the best of European Socialists often had to be paid for in the blood and suffering of the masses of the people.

Of course, on that warm day in July I could not foresee the future, but I remember that the meeting with Alvarez del Vayo left me with a sensation of vague inner alarm. One could not feel confident that Spanish democracy realised the danger that threatened it. And I felt even less confident that the democratic forces, including the Socialists, were taking really effective steps to avert that danger. . . .

In the rush and bustle of intervening events the feeling evoked by the conversation with Alvarez del Vayo gradually grew duller, was almost completely dispelled. A week later I was no longer thinking of Spain. And then on Sunday 19 July, on opening that day's issue of the *Observer*, I suddenly saw heavy headlines: 'Rebels Seize a Spanish City', 'Towns Bombed', 'Troops Being Rushed Up'.

Across my mind the thought flashed involuntarily: 'So much for Alvarez del Vayo's assurances!'

The next day, 20 July, even more alarming news from Spain appeared in the British press. The Conservative *Times* had column-headings like this:

'Civil War in Spain

A Monarchist Revolt

Rebels Control Morocco

Heavy Fighting'

beneath which the report ran:

'The "pure Republican" régime in Spain, established through the swing to the Left at the General Election of February, is

B

fighting for its life against a wide military revolt, described as openly Monarchist. The issue is still uncertain.'

The Labour *Daily Herald* said in its leading article:

'Spain is half-hidden behind the smoke-screen of civil war. And not until the screen is lifted will the world outside know fully what has happened and what is happening.

'But it is clear enough that the Republic has come to the crisis of its fate: and that on the outcome of these tragic days the whole future of the country hangs.

'The nature and purpose of the revolt are plain enough. It is a long-prepared, carefully planned attempt to overthrow the Constitution and to establish a ruthless military dictatorship.'

So the fears I had expressed in my conversation with Alvarez del Vayo proved perfectly well founded. But in their early stages events in Spain found no reflection in my work or life. I remained on the side-lines, as it were.

In the past I had never had any particular interest in Spain. To be honest, I did not know much about her. Paintings by Velazquez and Goya, the figures of Columbus and Cortes, the fires of the Inquisition, Cervantes' *Don Quixote*, the novels of Blasco Ibañez—there, in effect, you have all that would usually come into my mind at the mention of Spain. And this was no fortuitous fact. Throughout the centuries of their history the paths of Russia and Spain had not crossed at any point. The two countries had never come into any sort of contact, friendly or hostile. They went their separate ways, divided by what in those days were immense distances, and with no threads of political, economic or spiritual interaction to draw them together. Even in the age of Napoleon, when Russia and Spain were in fact on the same side, each carrying on a stubborn fight against Bonaparte's tyranny over the whole of Europe, there was little in common between them. True, in 1808, at the very beginning of the Spanish nation's fight against French invasion, the junta of Seville addressed an appeal for aid to the Russian Emperor Alexander I; but he remained deaf to it. True, four years later, in July 1812, after the break between Alexander and Napoleon, Russia and Spain concluded a treaty of military alliance; but the effect this had on the subsequent course of events was slight. True, the revolution of 1820–3 in Spain had a great influence on the Decembrist movement, but the tragic end of this movement also had its effect; in Russia the memory of the second Spanish revolution was gradually lost.

All these circumstances found their reflection in the destinies of Russian cultural development and Russian social thought during the 19th and 20th centuries. In those destinies Spain played practically no part. And from that fact flowed naturally enough the lack of interest in Spain on the part of our intellectuals. People were interested in Germany, interested in France, interested in England, interested in Italy, but Spain attracted the attention of no one except perhaps a few eccentrics. Right up to 1936 she occupied a very modest niche in international politics also. Nor were her home affairs striking or remarkable.

There was one further circumstance which had a moderating effect on my interest in Spanish affairs that summer. When Franco raised the banner of revolt in Morocco on 18 July, no one in Europe thought that the first battle of the second world war had begun and that the focus of world politics would shift to the Iberian peninsula for two whole years. On the contrary, everyone thought it would all be over very quickly. Franco himself was convinced that within 48 hours he would be master of Spain. The Republican government considered that it would crush the revolt within a few weeks at the most. Their belief in the rapid elimination of the revolt would have been justified, most probably, if it had not been for the intervention of Germany and Italy. But at the start of these events there were few who believed in the possibility of serious intervention on their part. It is doubtful whether even Hitler and Mussolini had any clear idea at that time of what the Spanish war would cost them. It is true that prior to 18 July they encouraged Franco in his intentions, and that in the first days of the revolt they sent him a small quantity of arms, a few dozen aircraft; they probably thought that beyond that they would scarcely be called on to do very much. It proved otherwise. Like a chain reaction, the first step involuntarily set in motion the next, then followed the third, fourth and so on, until they were sending whole armies of invasion to Spain, with hundreds of aircraft and thousands of guns. But in July no one could see all this . . .

In the summer of 1936, then, the prevailing opinion in European political circles was that the events in Spain were a purely internal struggle which should be over within a few weeks and which would not exert any appreciable influence on the international situation. I did not feel any confidence in the correctness of this prognosis. But as soon as the British Parliament adjourned and the close season for politics in London began, I decided, as usual, to go on leave. I asked permission to do so from Moscow. The Narkomindel (People's Commissariat for Foreign Affairs) had no objection, and in the middle of August 1936 my wife and I left England for seven weeks.

First we went to Sochi. Then we set out on a prolonged and extremely interesting journey through the Caucasus. And, to be frank, during that time I thought very little of Europe and all its acute and complex problems. Then, quite unexpectedly, I received a harsh reminder of the existence of Europe—that old, quarrelsome entity, rent asunder by its own contradictions!

2

Thoughts while travelling

DURING the day of 8 October I got back to Moscow. My wife's sister, who met us at the station, informed us that the telephone had been ringing non-stop for two days, with calls from the People's Commissariat of Foreign Affairs asking me to report immediately I returned to the Deputy People's Commissar for Foreign Affairs (the Commissar, M. M. Litvinov, was on leave at the time).

We had scarcely entered the flat when the telephone rang again. At the other end of the wire, it turned out, was the Deputy Commissar himself. He repeated once again the categoric demand that I go immediately to the People's Commissariat for Foreign Affairs.

Half an hour later we met. The Deputy Commissar greeted me with a hearty 'Well, thank God you're here at last!'

'What's the matter?' I enquired.

'Spain is the matter, Ivan Mikhailovich. . . . The things that are happening there are of great importance, and we cannot remain indifferent spectators. Our duty is to support the Spanish democrats. If victory goes to the Spanish Fascists, behind whom stand Germany and Italy, the danger of a European war will be increased. . . . In particular, it is extremely important to counteract by all possible means the dangerous machinations against the Spanish Republic that are going on at present in the London Committee for "Non-Intervention" in Spanish Affairs. It came into being after you had left on leave, but as our Ambassador in London you are a member of the Committee. . . . And since there is a sharp struggle going on inside it, you will have to speed up your return to London. . . .'

I began to enquire into all the details, and discovered that just before I had got back, on 7 October, the Soviet government had at a meeting of the Committee made a statement which must have far-reaching consequences. The Deputy People's Commissar gave it to me to read. The contents of the document showed that the U.S.S.R. was preparing to take decisive steps, capable of tearing apart the diplomatic cobweb of hypocritical 'non-intervention' which was so carefully being spun by the capitalist powers of Europe and America.

'You must leave for London tomorrow,' summed up the Deputy Commissar, 'and this evening you and I will be going to the Kremlin, where you will get precise instructions.'

At eleven o'clock that night we were indeed in the Kremlin. By then I had had time to familiarise myself with the entire correspondence on Spanish affairs between the Embassy in London and the People's Commissariat, and with the TASS agency's material on the same subject.

The meeting in the Kremlin did not last long. At it the Deputy People's Commissar for Foreign Affairs repeated more or less what he had said to me a few hours previously, and drew the final conclusion that the Soviet Ambassador in London must return forthwith to his post of duty. The discussion on this report was brief and to the point. The instructions I was given boiled down to this: the U.S.S.R. wanted peace and did not want war, the U.S.S.R. strove against aggressors everywhere and under all circumstances; this must be applied within the Committee for 'Non-intervention' also.

That was the general line. On the various particular questions which might arise, I was to ask for instructions telegraphically. At the same time I was expected to keep up attacking tactics in the Committee, since defensiveness could lead only to disaster.

I declared that I would act in accordance with instructions received, made my farewells and left.

By the evening of 9 October I was already sitting in a train which bore me swiftly westwards towards the Soviet-Polish border.

The journey from Moscow to London via Berlin and Paris took two days and three nights. All this time I was carefully preparing myself for the diplomatic battles ahead. I bought dozens of newspapers on the way, looking through them with special attention for everything that had any bearing on Spain. I talked to Soviet diplomats in Berlin and Paris about the positions of Germany and France. I thought out the possible moves and counter-moves in the Committee for 'Non-Intervention'.

What I wanted to do most of all was to succeed in discovering the main motive forces in the international situation as it had built up by October 1936. Many years of experience had convinced me that it is a poor diplomat who is too much concerned with evanescent, superficial 'current affairs'; he will be continually caught on the hop. In international politics there are big, deep, fundamental forces which in the last resort decide the course of events. Only if you know these forces can you steer a correct course in your everyday diplomatic work.

Gazing unseeingly at the towns and villages flashing past the carriage windows, I mentally reviewed the development of international relations since 1917. And this is what I made of it:

From the moment of the October Revolution the world was divided into two camps diametrically opposed in principle. In the twenty years that had passed since the Revolution two basic historical tendencies had made themselves quite clearly apparent: the camp of capitalism was on the decline, though more slowly than Soviet people had foreseen in the dawn of revolution; the world of socialism, on the contrary, was moving towards the zenith, though through greater difficulties and obstacles than the working people of our country expected when they took power into their hands. However, the leaders of the capitalist camp (and at that time this meant primarily the leaders of Britain, France and the U.S.A.) did not wish to recognise this objective truth (after all, no ruling class ever quits the stage without a bitter struggle), and were all the time attempting by various means to turn back the wheel of history. The means varied, but the aim remained the same.

At first—in the 1917–20 period—the leading lights of the capitalist camp tried to eliminate the bulwark of socialism, then still very weak, by using the 'big stick'—by supporting internal counter-revolution throughout Russia, by armed intervention. Then, having found that method a failure, they sought salvation in the possibility of eliminating socialism by the 'big money'— by trade and financial policies, by 'stick or carrot' diplomacy. That was their line in the twenties. But when this too failed to work and the u.s.s.r. started out on its Five-year Plans, which ensured a rapid growth of our material might, then the leaders of the capitalist camp returned once more to plans for the forcible suppression of the stronghold of socialism, though this time the plans took a rather different form.

In January 1933 the Nazis led by Hitler seized power in Germany. There was a split within the capitalist camp. Soon two groupings had taken shape: one, consisting of Germany, Italy and Japan, openly posed the question of a redivision of the world (including the capitalist part of it), while the other—Britain, France, the u.s.a.—being in control of the major part of the world's wealth, was in favour of maintaining the *status quo*. Striving to heal their schism and preserve a united front of the capitalist world against the socialist world, the leaders of capitalism (first and foremost in Britain, France and the u.s.a.) had the happy thought of reconciling their contradictions at the expense of the u.s.s.r. The statesmen in London, Paris and Washington contrived by various means to let it be understood by Hitler that he could seek *lebensraum* in the East without fear of opposition on their part, while they thought to themselves 'let the Germans and the Russians slaughter one another till they bleed to death, so much the better for us—there will be no danger to our positions in the world for a long time from either fascism or socialism'. Hitler was happy to take the hints of the 'democratic' powers about 'leaving him a free hand in the East', and he thought to himself 'now then, just where will it be most advantageous to begin redividing the world?'

So the net result was that the capitalist world was getting ready to use the 'big stick' against socialism once again, only this time the 'division of labour' between the various capitalist powers was rather different from what it had been in 1917–20.

That was how the general political line of the capitalist world looked in the years since 1933. All the other international questions troubling the different capitalist countries in those days were settled in strict dependence on that line. This came out with especial clarity in the behaviour of the 'democratic' powers. It was for the sake of maintaining that general line—the hope, that is, of bringing Germany and the u.s.s.r. into conflict in the East—that Britain, France and the u.s.a. allowed Germany to rearm frantically from 1935 on, and to re-militarise the Rhineland in 1936. It was for the same considerations that in 1935–6 Britain, France and the u.s.a. handed over little Ethiopia to be devoured by Fascist Italy.

Then the spearhead of Fascist aggression was turned against Spain. Why?

At that time I did not know much that has become known since. However, approaching the question from the point of view of common sense and political logic, I explained it thus:

In the summer of 1936, when the Spanish war began, Mussolini showed himself more 'dynamic' than Hitler. This was determined by the fact that at that time Germany was still in the early stages of rearmament, whereas Italy was already, within the limits of her abilities, 'ready for battle'. Her arms had been tested out in the Ethiopian war, and Mussolini, imagining himself a new Caesar, dreamed of the creation of a 'new Roman Empire' and of 'turning the Mediterranean into an Italian lake'. And how could he do that without setting a firm foot on the Iberian peninsula? Mussolini considered that it was that peninsula which must become the next objective of Fascist aggression.

Spain lay rather off the high road of German aggression, but at that stage the Nazi dictator had not yet completed his preparations for a second world war, and was prepared 'in the meantime' to support the plan of seizing the Iberian peninsula, so long as this would not demand too great an expenditure of strength and resources from Germany. Besides, Spain interested Hitler as a rich source of useful raw materials and, even more, as an important strategic position. Gaining control of that position would enable Germany to take France in the rear and to threaten, constantly and unavoidably, Britain's communications with the East. These would be trump cards in Hitler's hand when the second world war began. And, lastly, the victory of Fascism in yet another European country—and quite a considerable one at that—would go to raise the political prestige of Germany.

So it came about that the aims of the two Fascist dictators coincided, and the result was that on 18 July 1936 their puppet Franco raised his revolt against the Republican government of Spain.

How would the 'democratic' powers react to this new act of Fascist aggression? Would they sacrifice Spain as they had already sacrificed Ethiopia for the sake of their 'big play' with Hitler? Or would they on the contrary recognise that the map of Spain, with which so many economic and strategic considerations were linked, was too valuable to be thrown down without a struggle at the feet of the Fascist dictators?

Only the events of the immediate future could provide the answer to that question. But the first symptoms did not augur well. In none of the steps taken by Britain, France and the U.S.A. in connection with the Spanish war could one sense either firmness or decision. What I knew of the general political attitudes of British ruling circles caused me to doubt their desire and ability to cry 'Halt!' to the Fascist aggressors.

As we approached London I summed up my 'thoughts while travelling' as follows: First, one must expect Germany and Italy to be extremely brazen in their support of the Fascist revolt in Spain. Second, one must expect the 'democratic' powers, first Britain and France, to show cowardice (if no worse) in the struggle with German and Italian intervention.

These were the two basic propositions I had to take as my starting-point in my practical activity.

3

Getting acquainted with
the Committee for 'Non-intervention'

I ARRIVED in London on 12 October. It was a grey autumn
day. A sort of dull, dreggish wetness was falling from the sky.
At Victoria Station I was met by Counsellor of the Embassy
S. B. Kagan. During my absence he had been representing the
U.S.S.R. on the Committee for 'Non-intervention', and as soon
as we crossed the Embassy threshold he brought me up to date.
The picture that presented itself was most unattractive, even
threatening.

The idea of 'non-intervention' in Spanish affairs, on the basis
of which idea the Committee for 'Non-intervention' later arose,
was born in the depths of the British Foreign Office immediately
after the start of Franco's rebellion. The Spanish war put the
Baldwin government in a difficult position, since the decisive
part in the government was played by supporters of 'appeasement'. For reasons of which something has already been said, the
last thing this government wanted to do was quarrel with Hitler
over a mere Spanish Republic, which in any case they considered
'red', 'revolutionary', practically 'Communist'. But the broad
democratic masses in England and beyond its borders were
openly sympathetic to the Spanish Republic, and protested
loudly against intervention by Hitler and Mussolini on Franco's
side. So a compromise was called for, of the sort which would
protect the interests of both the sheep and the wolves.

The British Foreign Office found such a compromise, and the

Baldwin government gave it its blessing: Britain was to declare
its 'neutrality' in the Spanish war, thus avoiding the necessity of
being definitely on one side or the other. This would sound
respectable and even allow of appeals being made to the lofty
ideals of impartiality and justice. It could also be explained as
motivated by concern that the war should be localised and the
peace of Europe preserved. And lastly, it enabled Britain to
exert an ever-increasing influence on the final outcome of the
Spanish conflict, while conserving her own strength and without
quarrelling with Hitler.

However, to prevent a policy of this sort appearing too
repellent to the eyes of the democratic masses, in particular to
the British workers, the Baldwin government decided to impart
to it a more general, if possible, or European character. With
this object they addressed themselves first of all to France, where
a government of the *Front Populaire* was then in power, headed
by the Socialist Léon Blum. The latter was likewise an 'appeaser',
and greeted the British plan exceptionally sympathetically (for
the French workers were expressing their sympathy with the
Spanish Republic even more loudly and violently than their
British comrades). The result was that complete unity of views
on the Spanish question was immediately arrived at between the
French and British governments. And it was thereupon agreed,
in order that the democratic masses should be morally disarmed
more successfully, that the formal initiative in proposing an
agreement on 'non-intervention' should be taken not by the
Conservative Baldwin cabinet but by Blum's 'Socialist' government.

The position taken up by Britain and France was fully supported by the u.s.a. As we know, in 1935 the American Congress
had passed the Neutrality Act, which proclaimed that in the
case of war breaking out between third parties the President had
the right to ban the export of arms and war materials to the
warring countries, irrespective of whether a given country was
an aggressor or a victim of aggression. This Act was a real gift
to aggressors, who are always better and more heavily armed

than their opponents. But for the victims of aggression it was a stab in the back. The profoundly reactionary nature of the 'Neutrality' Act was made clear immediately after it had been passed, in the autumn of 1935, when it was first applied in practice in connection with the war between Italy and Ethiopia. Now this same Act coloured the whole attitude of the u.s.a. to the Spanish war. The support given by the American government ensured the success of the Anglo-French plans for 'non-intervention'.

So on 25 July 1936, just a week after Franco came out in the open, the Blum government issued a decree forbidding the export of arms from France to Spain. And on the first of August France addressed a Note to the British and Italian governments proposing that they associate themselves with the French action and strictly observe a policy of non-intervention in Spanish affairs.

On 4 August Britain returned a positive answer to the French proposal. On 6 August the Italian government did the same, though they accompanied their 'agreement in principle' with some very suspicious qualifications.

Then the French government addressed their proposal to other European powers (the Agreement was seen from the very beginning as taking in only the powers in Europe). On 17 August Germany responded. She expressed her readiness to join the common Agreement on non-intervention only if the u.s.s.r., Italy and Portugal also participated. On 23 August the Soviet government also joined the Agreement on non-intervention, but on condition that the Agreement should only come into force when Germany, Italy and Portugal had joined it.

On 26 August the French government put forward a new proposal: the creation in London of a permanent Committee of representatives of all the participant countries, the main aim of the Committee being supervision of the exact observance of the Agreement by the powers which had signed it. The French proposal was accepted, and a decision taken that the Committee for 'Non-intervention' should consist of the Ambassadors or envoys to London of the powers adhering to the Agreement. They were 27 in number.

Those on the Committee for 'Non-intervention' were: for Britain, the Earl of Plymouth, Parliamentary Under-Secretary to the Foreign Office; for France, Ambassador C. Corbin; for the U.S.S.R., Ambassador I. Maisky; for Germany, Ambassador J. Ribbentrop; for Italy, Ambassador D. Grandi; for Belgium, Ambassador Cartier de Marchienne; for Poland, Ambassador E. Raczyński; for Turkey, Ambassador Fethi Okyar; for Portugal, Ambassador A. Monteiro; for Czechoslovakia, Envoy J. Masaryk; for Austria, Envoy H. Franckenstein; for Hungary, Envoy C. Masirevich; for Greece, Envoy C. Simopoulos; for Bulgaria, Envoy S. Radov; for Roumania, Envoy B. Grigorcea; for Yugoslavia, Envoy S. Gruic; for Denmark, Envoy P. Ahlefeldt; for Norway, Envoy E. Colban; for Sweden, Envoy E. Palmstierna; for Finland, Envoy G. Gripenberg; for Holland, Envoy R. Swinderen; for Latvia, Envoy K. Zarin; for Estonia, Envoy A. Schmidt; for Lithuania, Envoy B. Balutis; for Luxemburg, Consul-General B. Klasen; for Albania, Chargé d'Affaires D. Duma; for Ireland, High Commissioner in London D. Dulanty.[1]

Only two of the states of Europe did not participate in the Committee: Spain, as the country around which the 'quarantine of non-intervention' was to be established, and Switzerland, which refused to participate in the Agreement on the grounds of her 'permanent neutrality'.

The non-European countries did not enter into either the Agreement or the Committee for 'Non-intervention'. In particular, the U.S.A. was not included. However, figuratively speaking its ghost was always present at the conference table, exerting the strongest of influences on the representatives of Britain, France and the other 'democratic' powers.

On 9 September 1936 the Committee for 'Non-intervention' gathered for its first meeting, and agreed that it should have a

1. In the course of the two and a half years for which the Committee existed there were of course some changes in its membership, but by and large it remained as given till its end.

permanent Chairman. This post was offered to the British representative, Lord Plymouth. . . .

But before passing on to a detailed consideration of the Committee's work I think it would not be out of place to elucidate precisely why the Soviet government adhered to the Agreement on 'Non-Intervention' in Spanish affairs. Viewing the whole history of the Committee now, retrospectively, I can say that the motives impelling the Soviet government at different periods during those two and a half years were not entirely the same.

In August 1936, when the Committee was only coming into being, two considerations were basic for the Soviet government:

First, the interests of peace. In our day any armed conflict, even a local one, carries with it the lurking threat of escalation into world war. The struggle then beginning in Spain was all the more pregnant with such danger.[1] It was necessary first of all to localise it and not allow the intervention of others, especially the Great Powers.

Secondly, the interests of democracy. The Soviet government understood that the broad masses of the Spanish people were for the Republic and that the rebels would soon fail, if only German and Italian intervention were prevented. It was therefore entirely logical to attempt, while not cherishing any Manilov-style illusions,[2] to achieve this prevention by means of an agreement on non-intervention.

Later on, when 'non-intervention' in Spanish affairs had shown itself to be an open farce, two other motives had arisen for the Soviet government's continued participation in the Agreement:

1. In a speech made on 28 September 1936 at a plenary session of the League of Nations the People's Commissar for Foreign Affairs, M. M. Litvinov, said: 'The Soviet government has associated itself with the Declaration on Non-Intervention in Spanish affairs only because a friendly power [i.e. France—I.M.] feared an international conflict if we did not do so' (see M. Litvinov, *Protiv Agressii (Against Aggression)* OGIZ, 1938, p. 30).

This was correct for the moment when the Blum government proposed that the U.S.S.R. should join the Agreement on Non-intervention.

2. See *Dead Souls*, by Gogol (trans.).

First, the interests of the fight to mobilise the democratic forces of the world to defend the Spanish Republic. The presence of Soviet representatives in the Committee for 'Non-intervention' afforded the opportunity of watching every move of the enemies of Spanish democracy, of exposing their intrigues, and of speaking to world public opinion of Fascism and the danger of war with full knowledge of what was going on.

Secondly, counteracting any international acts intended to worsen the position of the Spanish Republic. In the Committee for 'Non-intervention' the principle of unanimity obtained, as in the League of Nations, and this enabled the Soviet delegation by its single vote to kill in embryo many vicious machinations against Spanish democracy; not only the Fascist powers but the so-called 'democratic' powers also were greatly given to such things.

In the end the u.s.s.r. participated in the Agreement on 'Non-intervention' and in the Committee for the same almost until they ceased to exist. And in the light of history one can say boldly that this line of conduct fully justified itself.

From the notes of the meetings of the Committee which had taken place in my absence, and even more from S. B. Kagan's account of them, I was able to build up a preliminary idea of the moods and tendencies prevailing within this body. Little good was to be found. The Committee's practice in the first four or five weeks of its existence showed that its bourgeois members (particularly the Great Powers) were thinking not so much of carrying out the Agreement on Non-intervention as of sabotaging it.

At the very first meeting, when the question came up of how to plan the Committee's future work, the French representative Charles Corbin declared that 'the Committee should also, in our view, do everything to avoid debates of a political nature'.

So, the Blum government wanted there to be no political discussions in the Committee on the question which was then the quintessence of all that was most acutely political! It was like wanting hot ice or cold fire. But here was the most remarkable thing: none of the Committee's members representing the bourgeois countries uttered a word of objection or protest over such an absurdity.

At one of the subsequent meetings the Belgian representative, Baron Cartier de Marchienne, in speaking of the Committee's tasks, remarked meaningfully that it should be 'a modest committee of reconciliation, and should be content with such a role'. And again, the Belgian Ambassador's opinion was greeted with obvious approval by the majority of the Committee's members.

Translated into simpler terms, all this meant that the Committee should be like the ideal Japanese wife, who sees nothing, hears nothing and says nothing. And in fact, at a time when the press of the world was full of reports of the ceaseless stream of military advisers, complete with guns and aeroplanes, pouring in to Franco from Germany and Italy, the Committee at its first few meetings occupied itself making diplomatic spaghetti— empty academic arguments on subjects far from the practical needs of the moment. For hours on end they discussed such questions as: were gas-masks 'armaments' or were they not; was iron ore contraband or not; should non-European countries be brought into the Agreement on Non-intervention or should they not; should or should not the Agreement be extended to cover various forms of 'indirect intervention' in Spanish affairs (propaganda, collection of funds, etc.).

The following fact bears eloquent witness to the tendencies at work in the Committee in the direction of sabotaging real non-intervention. At the meeting of 14 September the British representative, W. S. Morrison, proposed that a Chairman's permanent Sub-committee should be set up, to consist of the delegates of those countries which were producers of armaments or which bordered on Spain. The official task of the Sub-committee was billed as the preparation of various questions for the full Committee, with all 27 countries party to the Agreement represented, to discuss later and decide upon. This proposal looked very innocent and even quite rational: who indeed could object to questions being presented to the plenary sessions not in the raw state, but partly worked over already, accompanied by the materials needed to make them better understood? But in actual fact the intention here was something entirely different. As soon as Morrison and Corbin had made their speeches supporting this proposal the suspicion came involuntarily to mind that Britain and France were trying to keep all matters connected with non-intervention within the narrowest possible circle, where everything could be discussed 'within the family'. For the same reasons Morrison insisted, when the decision to form a Sub-committee of nine members had been taken, that stenographic notes of the Sub-committee's meetings should not be made, only a brief record of decisions taken.[1]

Future practice fully confirmed the rightness of our suspicions.

To start with, the main activity of the Committee was concentrated in its plenary sessions. In the course of September and October 1936, there were 14 plenary sessions, while the Sub-committee met 17 times, and all its meetings at that period were in fact of a preparatory nature.

Later on the situation began to change: in 1937 there were 14 plenary sessions called, while the Sub-committee met 69 times. Now all the most important questions were being discussed and decided upon in the Sub-committee, and the plenary meeting was gradually turned into a voting machine which simply rubber-stamped the decisions taken by the Sub-committee.

In 1938 there were 17 meetings of the Sub-committee and only one plenary meeting.

The figures speak for themselves. It was perfectly obvious that not only Germany and Italy, but Britain and France as well, were trying to keep everything that had to do with the war in Spain as far away as possible from the eyes of world public opinion, including the eyes of the members of the Committee for 'Non-intervention'.

Another fact is no less significant. At the very first meeting of

1. Shorthand records of the Sub-committee's meetings were introduced much later, under circumstances which will be related below.

the Committee, on 9 September 1936, Morrison (again), on behalf of Britain, declared 'It is entirely for the Committee to decide . . . for my part, I would suggest that we get on very well in private.'

And once again not one of the members of the Committee representing a bourgeois country said a word in opposition. The result was a decision that at the end of each meeting there would be only a short official communiqué, which was to be of as 'general' a character as possible, that is, was to say nothing.

The Soviet side, however, had quite another point of view. It held that the work of the Committee should proceed with the widest possible publicity, and therefore after the first meeting it informed British journalists in detail of all that had taken place. The next day, 10 September, alongside the official communiqué there appeared unofficial but very circumstantial reports. This aroused strong feeling among some of the Committee's members. At the next meeting, on 14 September, Morrison expressed regret at what had happened and appealed once more to all taking part in the Committee to preserve the secrecy of its work. The British delegate was supported by the representatives of Germany and Italy. Especially agitated was the Italian Ambassador Grandi, who complained that the press accounts 'completely distorted' his government's position, and categorically demanded that the Committee's meetings should remain secret.

This question of the 'leakage' of information from the four walls of the Committee became a constant sore point at all the plenary sessions and Sub-committee meetings. I had from time to time to fight off attacks on this score on the part of the Great Powers' representatives, especially those of Britain, Germany and Italy. At last things blew up to a major row, which took place at the meeting of the Sub-committee on 7 May 1937.

The British representative, Lord Plymouth, took it on himself to fire the opening shot. He made a long speech, in which he turned the full force of his wrath upon the wretched 'informers' and declared in the most categorical language that Britain could not allow the Committee to be turned into 'an instrument of propaganda'. Plymouth proposed a resolution, to be given the widest possible publicity, that the sole objective source of information on the work of the Committee was to be found in the communiqués which it regularly issued.

The Italian Ambassador, Grandi, hastened to Plymouth's support and let fly a few shafts in the direction of the Soviet side. We however treated these with unruffled composure, and this evoked a violent reaction from Ribbentrop. He uttered a real corporal-style tirade against 'Soviet propaganda' and proposed that a special commission be set up 'to seek out the culprits' guilty of constant leakage of information and 'work out measures that could be taken to prevent such happenings in the future'.

The example of the 'Big Three' was followed by some of their supporting voices.

There was a great deal of noise, but the mountain brought forth only a mouse. Since the unanimity principle obtained in the Committee, Plymouth did not even go to the length of putting Ribbentrop's proposal to the vote. No measures against leakage of information were taken. And the Soviet side, enduring calmly the latest of many attacks, continued to supply the press with truthful information on the activities of the Committee for 'Non-intervention'.

The firmness of the u.s.s.r. on making public the work of the Committee bore good fruit. On 28 October 1937 the Committee decided to publish in future detailed information bulletins after each meeting of the Sub-committee, and that 'in exceptional cases there should be attached thereto the full text of such declarations made by individual delegates'. Afterwards the qualifying clause about 'exceptional cases' somehow disappeared of its own accord, and the most important speeches made by members of the Committee were regularly issued to the press after each meeting. This made it immeasurably easier for the friends of the Spanish Republic to mobilise the democratic forces of the world in its defence. The veil of secrecy had been torn from the Committee and its Sub-committee, and their activities revealed to a wide public in all their repellent nastiness . . .

But I run on too quickly. In the middle of October 1936, when I returned to London from Moscow, the questions on the agenda were rather different. But before proceeding to describe the diplomatic battles which the Soviet side had to fight out in the Committee and Sub-committee during the winter of 1936-7 I must pause awhile to consider the situation within Spain as it had then taken shape.

4

Revolution and counter-revolution

IN THE course of the 19th century Spain lived through five revolutions.[1] They were very prolonged and complex but in essence they came down to a struggle for power between the old feudal landed estates and the bourgeoisie then gradually coming into existence. But owing to the slow and feeble growth of capitalist development in the country the Spanish bourgeoisie was not sufficiently strong to win a decisive victory over its opponent, as had happened in neighbouring France, for instance. The result was that all five revolutions remained incomplete. In the course of them the bourgeoisie succeeded in winning some secondary positions in the apparatus of power, but the decisive force in the state remained, as before, the landowners.

After an interval of almost half a century the sixth Spanish revolution broke in 1931. Essentially it was even now a matter of eliminating first of all the still numerous remnants of feudalism. But the sixth Spanish revolution was taking place in the era of imperialism, when the big bourgeoisie everywhere (including Spain) had become a reactionary force, and the petty bourgeoisie a spineless and vacillating entity. It was also of immense importance that before the sixth revolution in Spain came the October Revolution in Russia, that the proletariat everywhere (including Spain) had come forward on the historical stage as the class to which the future belonged. In this setting the sixth Spanish revolution (even in its bourgeois-democratic aspect)

1. *Viz.* the revolutions of 1808–14, 1820–3, 1833–43, 1854–6 and 1868–74.

could be victorious only under the leadership of the proletariat, after which the process of 'growing into' a revolution of a higher type would have commenced naturally. But the essential premise for such a course of development was the unity of the proletariat and the existence of a strong Communist Party at its head.

What, however, was the actual state of affairs at the moment of commencement of the sixth revolution?

By way of legacy from the past the Spanish working class had inherited a deep schism of 60 years standing, the split between Anarchists and Socialists (and Socialists of a very opportunistic variety at that). The Spanish Communist Party was still very weak. The result was that for the first five years of the revolution (1931–5) power was in the hands of parties and people who were either incapable of getting rid of the survivals from feudalism and bringing the country out on to the high road of Socialist development, or quite simply hostile to any such idea. Only in 1936, when the Communist Party had grown stronger, and later under the influence of wartime conditions, was a situation in being which opened up more favourable prospects for Spain. But here a new factor came into play—foreign intervention— which was fated to play a disastrous role in Spanish history for the second time.[1]

But we will not run ahead too fast. Let us trace the path of the sixth Spanish revolution step by step from its very beginning.

For the first two years (1931–3) power belonged to a *bloc* comprising the petty-bourgeois parties of Left Republicans and the Socialist Party of Spain. This *bloc*, led by the Left Republican Azaña and the Socialists Largo Caballero and Indalecio Prieto, carried out a number of half-hearted reforms (in the political, agrarian and ecclesiastical fields), but could not make up its mind to deal a fatal blow at the relics of feudalism. The situation was particularly bad as regards the solution of the most important

1. The Spanish revolution of 1820–3 was also crushed by armed intervention, by the so-called 'Holy Alliance', by whose decision and in whose name France sent her armies into Spain to restore Ferdinand VII to the throne.

internal problem Spain possessed—the land question. The agrarian reform announced by the government at the end of 1932 was so timid in nature and so slow in being applied that if the same rate of progress had been maintained about a thousand years would have been required for its final completion!

The result of this was that the Republican-Socialist *bloc* fell between two stools. Both Right and Left were dissatisfied. The masses of the people, disillusioned by the paucity of the benefits they were reaping, began to turn their backs on the *bloc*. This was seized on by the Right, united in CEDA[1] of unblessed memory.

Led by the conservative and Catholic Gil Robles, CEDA had made skilful use of the machinery of parliamentarism and of the split in the Left, and had succeeded in winning the 1933 elections with the aid of money and brute force; the intention was to restore the old order in Spain. But the revolutionary spirit of the masses—the Spanish workers and peasants—was too great, and CEDA suffered defeat before achieving its aim. The famous Asturian rising in October 1934, and the parliamentary elections in February 1936, which brought victory to the National Front,[2] showed that a dictatorship of landowners and capitalists was impossible.

The Left Republicans again came to power, under the same Azaña. They were supported by the Socialists and the Communists. It was at this point, having lost their parliamentary positions, that the Right decided to go over to military, Fascist methods of struggle. In these they were given every support by Germany and Italy, who had an extensive network of agents throughout the country.

During the night before 18 July 1936 Ceuta radio sent out into the ether the message 'Over all Spain the sky is cloudless'. This was the agreed signal for the start of the revolt. The conspirators'

1. CEDA is the name by which was known the Spanish Confederation of Autonomous Rightist Parties, formed in February 1933 (from the initials of its title—*Confederación Español de derechos autonomos*).

2. The People's Front in Spain united the most various parties, from the Communists to the Radicals.

plans provided for simultaneous Fascist rebellions in the army in different parts of continental Spain, under the command of Generals Mola, Queipo de Llano and others, also in Morocco, where the leader of the revolt was to be General Franco. The leaders of the revolt had the greatest contempt for the masses of the people, and were sure that in the course of 48 hours they would succeed in overthrowing the Republican government and taking power into their own hands.

On 18 July rebellion did indeed flare up in various parts of the country, but only in Morocco, Navarre, Seville and a few other areas was it successful. On the contrary, in the majority of the big towns the rebels suffered defeat; in Madrid and Barcelona they were simply wiped out. The explanation was that all over the country the people spoke out clearly.

It cannot be maintained that on the side of the people there at once appeared leaders of sufficient farsightedness. No; regrettably, this did not happen. The Left Republican government of Jiral, which had assumed power at the very beginning of the rebellion, opened the arsenals to arm the people, which was of course very good, but they were quite obviously too late with their formation of a new Republican army. The decree on this was issued only on 21 August, i.e. a month after the revolt, although everyone could see that the army inherited from the monarchy was in the main on the side of the rebels. Another of the government's obvious miscalculations was their attempt to create the new army on the basis of old officers who for one reason or another had not gone over to Franco.

The Jiral government had neither authority nor skill enough to bring any real organisation into the mass struggle which the workers and peasants everywhere spontaneously put up against the Fascist military conspirators. The result was that elements of organisation began to be contributed by different parties and groups, and since there were very many of these, often in competition with one another, the Spanish democrats' fight against Fascism was for a long time in a chaotic state. They had not enough arms, enough officers, they had not enough experience, training, military knowledge, or operational liaison between different units. In addition, the Jiral government for some reason believed that Britain would not allow the establishment of Fascist rule in Spain, and in consequence gave a quite unjustified bias to the Republic's foreign policy.

None the less, though, Spanish democracy put up a mighty resistance to the rebels, and would of course have quickly crushed them if the Fascist-minded generals had not been supported by external forces.

When the conspirators realised that their plans for a lightning victory had gone astray they began to prepare, aided by their German and Italian allies, a 'march on Madrid'. According to the plan they worked out, the attack on the Spanish capital was to be carried out by two columns—one from the south, from Seville, under the command of General Mola, and one from the north, from Navarre, under General Franco. At this stage the rebels still believed in a speedy end to the struggle; if they had not seized power within 48 hours, at least they would do so in 3 or 4 weeks.

However, in putting into effect the plan they had worked out they met with great difficulties. The population as a rule met the rebel troops with hostility. The Republican militia, poorly trained and badly armed, but burning with revolutionary enthusiasm, put up a stubborn resistance. When General Mola's troops drew close to the Guadarrama and Somosierra, a mountain ridge 40–50 kilometres from Madrid, there was heard everywhere the famous slogan *No pasarán!* ('They shall not pass!'). Units of the people's militia hastened to the threatened points. In buses, lorries, cars and carts, on mules, donkeys and on foot they made their way in a mighty flood to the mountain passes, and almost literally closed these with their bodies. The losses of the militia were enormous, but Mola's advance was beaten back.

Franco occupied Córdoba and Badajoz, which he drowned in Republican blood. But he too found he could advance no further. The revolt was clearly running out of impetus, and if Spain had been left to her own devices the Republic would have been victorious by the second half of August.

Hitler and Mussolini were alarmed. They had never imagined such an outcome possible. German and Italian aid to the rebels was stepped up; the numbers of aircraft, tanks and guns sent to them were increased. A large force of Fascist warships was concentrated in Spanish waters, including the German battleship *Deutschland*.

At the same time 'non-intervention' reared its ominous head; the Republic began to come up against unexpected difficulties in obtaining arms from abroad. The majority of Ambassadors accredited to the Spanish government (in particular, those of Britain and France) left Madrid and took up temporary residence in Hendaye, a small town on the Franco-Spanish border. There the web was spun of all manner of intrigues against the Spanish Republic. And in the capital, where only secondary diplomatic officials remained, the premises of a number of Embassies (especially those of the Latin-American countries) were transformed into real centres of counter-revolution. On these premises, under the protection of diplomatic immunity, thousands of rebels were hidden, and centres for espionage and diversionary activities set up by the right-wing parties.

Such manifold aid afforded to counter-revolution from outside could not but find reflection in the situation of the Republic. From the second half of August, and particularly in September, the position at the fronts began to worsen. On 2 September Irun fell; on the 4th the rebels occupied Talavera (120 kilometres from the capital), and on the 27th they took Toledo (70 kilometres from the capital).

On 30 September Franco was proclaimed, in Burgos, head of a 'national government', and Generalissimus. On 4 October Seville radio announced that the rebels were starting to surround Madrid.

Two days later the same radio station boastfully asserted that the Spanish capital would be occupied by the rebels on 12 October. General Mola, who was still unable to break through across the Guadarrama and Somosierra, was told to keep as many Republican troops as possible tied up there.

Immediately after the fall of Irun and Talavera, the Left Republican Jiral government resigned, and a coalition government under Largo Caballero came to power. This government included representatives of all the parties of the People's Front— Socialists, Communists, petty-bourgeois republicans of various persuasions, Basques, Catalans, and at one time Anarchists as well.

On 1 October the new government passed through the Cortes a law giving the Basques their autonomy, thus solving one of the most acute internal problems of Spain. On 7 October, at the instance of the Communist Minister for Agriculture, Uribe, a decree was issued for the confiscation of lands from 'enemies of the Republic'. This decree virtually wiped out large landed estates, since almost all the landowners were enemies of the Republic. The confiscated land was nationalised and given, via specially created land committees, to the peasants. In some places co-operatives began to come into existence. All this was of immense political and military importance.

At the same time the Republic took energetic measures of a purely defensive nature, though here the new Premier and Minister for War, Largo Caballero, was far from rising fully to the situation. His blunders were to some extent put right by the Communist Party and the famous Fifth Regiment it had created.[1]

A start was made on building around Madrid a triple ring of fortifications, at distances of 20–35, 12–14 and 6–8 kilometres from the city centre. But Largo Caballero for some reason thought that fortifications of all kinds only demoralised an army, so only the third ring, running through the actual suburbs of the city, was successfully completed. The other two belts remained as they were, unfinished.

1. The Fifth Regiment was brought into being by the Communist Party during the very first days of the rebellion, and became a forcing-house for leaders of the future Republican army. It formed and trained new units, gave them arms, gave them officers, carried on wide agitational and propaganda work. In five months of its existence the Fifth Regiment produced 70,000 soldiers for the Republic. At the beginning of 1937 it became the framework on which could be built up the country's new armed forces.

5

The U.S.S.R. defines
its position precisely

I T W A S 23 October when I first found myself at a meeting
of the Committee. It was a plenary meeting and all 27 members
were present. It took place in the Locarno Room, as it was
known, of the Foreign Office, where 11 years earlier the Locarno
Agreements had been signed.[1]

On the far side of the table, dead centre, facing the entrance,
towered the massive figure of the Committee's Chairman, Lord
Plymouth. To his right and left were the Secretaries, Francis
Hemming and Roberts. They were whispering all the time with
Plymouth about something.

The other members of the Committee were ranged around the
outer edge of the table in alphabetical order of the names of
their countries (English spelling). My neighbour on the left
proved to be the Swedish Ambassador Baron Erik Palmstierna,
with whom I had long been on good terms. On my right hand
sat the Yugoslav envoy Slavko Gruic—a man little known to me
(in those years there were still no diplomatic relations between
the u.s.s.r. and Yugoslavia, and I only rarely met Gruic at
official receptions given by the British). Opposite me, on the

1. These Agreements were concluded in 1925 as a result of talks between
Great Britain, France, Germany, Italy, Belgium, Czechoslovakia and
Poland. Their avowed aim was to guarantee Germany's western frontiers,
but in fact they signified a re-grouping of forces among the imperialist
powers for the creation of an anti-Soviet *bloc*.

other side of the table, was the place of the Italian representative
Dino Grandi, and a little to his left sat Germany's representative.
She was to be represented by Joachim Ribbentrop, who had a
short time previously been appointed Ambassador to Britain.
But Ribbentrop was not yet in London, and his place on the
Committee was being taken by Counsellor of the German
Embassy Prince Bismarck (a descendant of the 'Iron Chancellor').

Every member of the Committee was accompanied by a deputy
or a secretary. There were numerous experts. Altogether nearly
a hundred people were present at the meeting. But there was a
strange hush in the hall. The majority of those present preferred
to keep silent. And if anyone did talk, it was only quietly or even
in a whisper, as at the bedside of someone seriously ill.

The meeting was opened by Lord Plymouth in the following
words: 'Your Excellencies and Gentlemen, before I read out to
the Committee a letter which I have received from His Excellency
the Soviet Ambassador, I would like to make a statement on
behalf of His Majesty's government bearing upon the work of
this Committee in general . . .'

Plymouth went on to repeat the stereotyped declarations about
the aim of the British government in supporting the Agreement
on Non-intervention being to 'prevent the civil war from
spreading beyond the Spanish frontiers', about the task of the
Committee being to supervise the exact observance of the Agreement by all its members, and this only being possible given
'frank co-operation' between those governments participating in
the Agreement, and about the duty of the Committee's members
being, in considering complaints of infringement of the Agreement, to act 'in an impartial spirit and with the firm intention
of excluding any political considerations which may endanger
the realisation of the common aim'.

This speech of Plymouth's reminded me of Chekhov's 'The
Volga flows into the Caspian Sea, horses eat oats and hay'. But
the other members of the Committee took it (outwardly at
least), if not as a revelation of divine truth, then at any rate as a
kind of obligatory prayer before sleep.

But at last the 'prayer' was over, and Plymouth reached the main attraction of the day, which proved to be the letter, already mentioned, which he had received from me dated 23 October. To make things clearer a few preliminary observations are needed here.

The reader has already had the opportunity of seeing something of the metaphorical spillikin-picking to which the Committee had devoted itself with such enthusiasm in the first weeks of its existence. But the U.S.S.R. was not inclined to take part in such pastimes. As early as 7 October S. B. Kagan had, on instructions from the Soviet government, presented Plymouth with a statement which caused great confusion in the Committee. In this document, based mainly on materials furnished by the Republican government of Spain, was listed a series of gross violations by Portugal of the Agreement on Non-intervention, after which followed the conclusion:

'The Soviet government fears that such a situation . . . renders the Agreement on Non-Intervention non-existent in practice. The Soviet government can in no circumstances agree to the turning of the Agreement on Non-Intervention into a screen concealing military aid from some of the participants in the Agreement to the rebels, against the legitimate government of Spain. The Soviet government is obliged, in view of this, to declare that unless violations of the Agreement on Non-Intervention cease forthwith, it will consider itself as freed from the obligations arising from the Agreement.'

At the Committee's plenary meeting on 9 October, when this statement was discussed, the Portuguese representative Calheiros (taking the place of the Ambassador Monteiro, who had not yet arrived in London) was demonstratively absent, but the Italian representative Grandi made one of his blood-and-thunder speeches against the U.S.S.R.; S. B. Kagan returned him a deservedly sharp answer. The final result was that the Committee, at Plymouth's suggestion, decided to request the Portuguese government to furnish explanations on the accusations made against it.

On 12 October, the day of my return to London, S. B. Kagan, on instructions from the People's Commissariat for Foreign Affairs, sent Plymouth a fresh letter, insisting that the British and French fleets must establish a watch on Portuguese ports. Plymouth replied that he did not consider it reasonable to summon the Committee together to discuss this proposal before it had received the explanations offered by the Portuguese government. An obvious playing for time had begun . . .

But here something very germane to the issue occurred. On 16 October there was published a telegram sent by the Central Committee of our Party to the Secretary of the C.C. of the Communist Party of Spain. This read: 'The working people of the Soviet Union are only doing their duty in rendering what aid they can to the revolutionary masses of Spain. They are fully aware that the liberation of Spain from the yoke of the Fascist reactionaries is not a private concern of Spaniards, but the common cause of all forward-looking and progressive humanity. Fraternal greetings!'[1]

Thus the general line of the u.s.s.r. in relation to events in Spain had been proclaimed openly. On this basis the People's Commissar for Foreign Affairs, M. M. Litvinov, had instructed me to make a further statement and to take another step forward in making the position of the Soviet government absolutely clear. It was this statement which I had sent in written form to Lord Plymouth on the morning of 23 October.

We recalled the systematic violation of the Agreement on Non-intervention by 'a number of its participants', including Portugal, as a result of which 'a privileged situation for the rebels has been created', while 'the legitimate government of Spain has turned out to be in fact under boycott, deprived of facilities to purchase arms outside Spain for the defence of the Spanish people'. The statement went on to note that all the efforts of the Soviet government's representative to put an end to violations of the Agreement had found no support in the Committee, and from this drew the conclusion 'Thus the Agree-

1. *Izvestia*, 16 October 1936.

ment has turned out to be an empty, torn scrap of paper. It has ceased in practice to exist. Not wishing to remain in the position of persons unwittingly assisting an unjust cause, the Government of the Soviet Union sees only one way out of the situation created: to return to the Spanish Government the right and facilities to purchase arms outside of Spain. . . .

'In any case, the Soviet Government, unwilling to bear any longer the responsibility for the clearly unjust situation created in regard to the legitimate Spanish Government and the Spanish people, is compelled now to declare that in accordance with its statement on 7 October, it cannot consider itself bound by the Agreement for Non-Intervention to any greater extent than any of the remaining participants of the Agreement.'

The sense of the statement just quoted was perfectly clear: the U.S.S.R. would observe the Agreement on Non-intervention only if violations of the Agreement on the part of Germany, Italy and Portugal ceased. But in the measure that the Fascist powers, while remaining members of the Committee, continued to intervene in Spanish affairs in the interests of reaction and war, the U.S.S.R. had no option but to do the same in the interests of peace and democracy.

Thus the Soviet government did not let itself be caught in the fowler's net of the paragraphs and articles and legal forms of the Agreement, and by so doing miss the essence of the matter. . . .

When he had read out the Soviet declaration, Plymouth shrugged his shoulders as if mystified, saying: 'I think that I should now ask the Soviet Ambassador whether he desires to say anything in explanation of the letter which was handed to me on his behalf. . . . It seems to me that it contains phrases which are somewhat difficult actually to construe or interpret. . . .'

Grandi also addressed much the same question to me. It was clear that both of them wanted to catch me out on some careless word. What a frenzied dance of the cannibals the Fascist papers would have started up then, and many of the 'democratic' ones too! However, I deprived them of that pleasure. My answer was

D

to parry—'I have nothing to add to the text of the letter. I think that the letter is sufficiently clear, and that the consequences are quite obvious.'

Sensing that no more was to be got out of me, Plymouth proposed that discussion of the Soviet statement be transferred to the Sub-committee and the next point on the agenda taken, which was the answers of Germany, Italy and Portugal to the complaints received by the Committee of violations by them of the Agreement on Non-intervention. . . .

Here again I shall have to give a few explanatory remarks.

The Soviet government's statement of 7 October had found a wide and favourable response in democratic circles in Britain and elsewhere. A sigh of relief went up: at last a government had been found which, tearing apart the veil of diplomatic hypocrisy, honestly stated its intentions.

The British workers were openly sympathetic to us, and this could not but find its reflection within the Labour Party. For the first six weeks of the Spanish war the Labour leaders remained obstinately silent, avoiding the adoption of any clearly defined attitude. Only when further silence became impossible did they summon, on 28 August, a meeting of the Labour Members of Parliament, the Party executive, and the General Council of the T.U.C., at which it was decided:

First, to maintain a policy of neutrality in the Spanish war.

Secondly, to resist the running of a mass campaign in support of Republican Spain (which the Communists were insisting on).

The leadership of the British labour movement thus allied itself, in effect, with the policy of 'non-intervention' being followed by the British government.

Two weeks later, on 10 September, the Trades Union Congress in Plymouth endorsed the resolution of 28 August. A motion to reject it was lost by a majority of 3,029 thousand against 51 thousand.[1]

1. The voting system at Trades Union Congresses is highly undemocratic. In essence it is as follows: it is not the delegates who vote, but their unions; each trade union has a fixed, previously established number of

The chief argument which the Labour and trade union leaders advanced in support of their attitude was the danger of the Spanish war being transformed into a general European conflict. In the tense atmosphere of those years this argument was convincing enough for a considerable part of the British (and not only the British) proletariat.

However, the nearer the rebels drew to Madrid and the more obvious the intervention of the Germans and Italians on Franco's side became, the higher rose the wave of protest against 'non-intervention' among the British and French workers. From 5 to 9 October the Labour Party's annual conference was in session in Edinburgh. The Soviet government statement which has been quoted above came in the middle of its deliberations. This *démarche* on our part aroused a fresh outburst of indignation in proletarian circles against the blockade of the Spanish Republic. The masses were plainly ready to do battle, which did not suit the leadership of the Labour Party at all. But the impression made by the Soviet statement of 7 October was too great, and the Edinburgh conference could not ignore it. The Labour bosses began to manœuvre: the Leader of the Labour party, Attlee, and his deputy Greenwood visited the Prime Minister and demanded urgent investigation of all accusations regarding the violation by some powers of the Agreement on Non-intervention, and, in the event of such violations being established, that the Republican government of Spain be accorded the right to buy arms abroad. The meeting with the Prime Minister was reported to the Conference, which considered itself satisfied and passed the final

votes, depending on the numbers of members it has; if within the delegation of a trade union disagreements arise, only the opinion of the majority is taken into account (the votes of the minority do not count). An example: let us suppose that a trade union has 50 votes, and that within its delegation, which numbers 60, there are 31 'for' and 29 'against' a particular resolution put forward by the General Council; when the final count is taken all 50 votes of that union will be considered as having been given in favour of the resolution. Thanks to this system, known as the 'block vote', the leadership of the T.U. movement is often successful in getting decisions passed regardless of opposition views.

decision of the Party's line on the 'Spanish question' over to the Executive. And the latter, after the Conference, 'found no justification' for any change in its previous position.

So the leadership of the Labour Party sabotaged the true feelings of the masses. This was repeated, regrettably, on subsequent occasions. Throughout the whole course of the Spanish war the Labour Party as a whole (I am not speaking of the individual honourable exceptions) played a treacherous role towards Republican Spain, and its example was followed by other socialist parties. And now, many years later, looking back over the events of those days, one sees with singular clarity what a large share of responsibility for the triumph of Fascism in Spain must be borne by the Second International . . .

The British cabinet too had to manœuvre. On 9 October Lord Plymouth on behalf of his government raised in the Committee a complaint of infringement of the Agreement by the Fascist powers. This complaint was based on the very same materials from the Spanish Republican government which had figured in the Soviet declaration of 7 October; and according to the accepted procedure it was sent to Germany, Italy and Portugal with a request that an explanation be furnished. The answers of the governments concerned had been received in time for the meeting of 23 October, and the Chairman, Plymouth, after an unsuccessful attack upon myself, proposed that we proceed to the consideration of these replies.

The German reply was taken first. It consisted of two parts: in the first of these the Berlin government categorically and flatly rejected all the accusations made against it; and in the second it advanced a whole series of accusations itself against the U.S.S.R. And at this point the tactics of the British side made themselves apparent. I cannot assert that all that took place during the rest of that meeting was pre-agreed beforehand between Plymouth and Bismarck (I would say myself that there was no formal understanding). But their souls were in harmony to such an extent that all through the meeting Prince and Lord played the same tune very smoothly.

Plymouth moved that the German reply be taken point by point: complaint so-and-so, answer so-and-so. It was difficult to make any objection to such a method. Everyone agreed to it.

Plymouth first of all asked Bismarck whether he wished to add anything to the written reply of the German government. The German representative said that he had 'little to add' to the document received from Berlin, and only stressed particularly that the greater part of the accusations contained in the British complaint referred to things which had taken place before Germany had signed the Agreement on Non-intervention.

Plymouth eagerly seized on Bismarck's words and for quite a long while chewed them over in varying combinations. The net result was that the German government was really entirely innocent. True, Plymouth added, the British complaint did contain, besides the accusations founded on Spanish materials, some others based on facts from purely British sources . . . Here the speaker made a slight pause and, looking meaningly at Bismarck, enquired '. . . whether Prince Bismarck is in a position to throw any light on those points?'

Bismarck was only too ready to oblige, and declared roundly that 'all the accusations were entirely without foundation', though if the Committee's Chairman wished, he was prepared to ask his government for additional explanations on the points indicated. And at this the German representative made the most courteous of gestures in Plymouth's direction.

Plymouth enquired of those present 'Does anyone wish to make any observations?'

There was no one who did. This was typical of the Committee. As a rule only the representatives of the five Great Powers took part in discussion—the members for Britain, France, the u.s.s.r., Germany and Italy. All the others either kept silent or discharged their obligations by uttering remarks of no significance, usually relating to procedural questions. In this case Grandi and Corbin also found it unnecessary to say anything. The former because Plymouth's behaviour did not threaten any unpleasantness for his German colleague, and the latter in general was mainly concerned that there should be no 'rows' on the Committee.

I then asked leave to speak myself, and subjected the German answer to devastating criticism. Particularly categorical were my remarks taking exception to the attempts by the German side to reject all the accusations against her without substantiating her case in any way.

Plymouth hastened to Bismarck's aid. Announcing that he was going to approach the matter 'from a purely judicial standpoint', the Chairman expended a good deal of energy to prove that the facts which I adduced as incriminating the German government had occurred before Germany joined the Committee. Plymouth concluded his speech with his usual refrain: 'I should be very grateful if anybody would express any view on this discussion . . .'

Again there was no one who wanted to do so. Plymouth recorded the fact with an appearance of regret, and immediately moved that advantage should be taken of Prince Bismarck's kind offer to request the German government for information on some points that were not yet entirely cleared up.

I strongly opposed his motion. It meant only a further delay in the Committee's passing judgment on a matter of great urgency. 'Personally,' I added, 'I find the German reply unsatisfactory.'

It was clear, of course, that the Committee would not support me. None the less I insisted on an immediate decision. My calculation was a simple one: a vote against the British complaint would be one more striking fact bearing witness to the uselessness of the Agreement on Non-intervention, and would serve to expose the whole farce put up by the British and French 'appeasers'.

The firm stand taken by the Soviet side had its result: a decision was taken immediately. Putting on an expression of impartial impenetrability, like Themis with her eyes bound, Plymouth announced: '. . . the German reply, in my view, must be taken as dealing satisfactorily with the incidents alleged . . . That is not the view taken by the Soviet representative, but . . .'

The Chairman shrugged his shoulders expressively, as if to finish the unspoken '. . . but that is his affair', and then went on to develop the idea that in general complaints of infringement of the Agreement on Non-intervention 'in the first instance at any rate, can be more properly discussed by the Chairman's Sub-committee'. All those present were silent, casting down their eyes. No one expressed disagreement, although some members of the Committee, as I learnt later, did not at all like the line taken by the Chairman. But that was the custom that had grown up in the Committee from the very beginning of its work . . .

The wordless silence reigning over the table angered me, and I addressed a question to Plymouth: 'May I ask what you find in the German reply that is satisfactory? Is it the essence of the reply, the explanations given, or the form of the reply?'

Plymouth blinked uncertainly and replied rather hesitantly: 'I am afraid that I find it a little difficult to appreciate these distinctions. I do not really know what the object of that question was.'

I went on even more sharply: 'I would like you to elucidate in what way you find the German reply satisfactory.'

At this point Roberts, the Assistant Secretary, who sat on Plymouth's right, whispered something in his ear. Plymouth suddenly reddened, jerked his head angrily, and exclaimed in an entirely different tone: 'Really, I am not here to be cross-examined by members of the Committee. It seems to me that you have to form your own judgment and your own view on the evidence before you.'

It was clear that Roberts had 'gingered up' Plymouth (this was often to be repeated in the future), and the latter had rushed in to the attack like a bull, head down.

To ward off Plymouth's attack I raised the question of a naval check on Portuguese ports. A Note about this had been sent to the Committee by S. B. Kagan on 12 October. In few but forceful words I stressed the extreme urgency of this question.

Plymouth went over to the defensive at once. He began to demonstrate that there was no irrefutable proof of Portugal's guilt, that in any case one should not pick on one country as a scapegoat, but should think of measures of a more general nature.

Corbin supported Plymouth's proposal to transfer the question of Portugal to the Sub-committee. The same opinion was expressed by the Belgian representative, Baron Cartier de Marchienne. Then the Dutch representative Baron van Swinderen rose and, trying to put as much warmth and feeling into his voice as possible, turned to me with an earnest request not to demand the immediate consideration of the Portuguese question, for according to the accepted procedure one should first consider the replies of the Italian and Portuguese governments, and then decide what to do next. This was one more attempt to put off indefinitely a matter that permitted of no delay, and I could not stop my blood boiling. With a sharpness which would really have been better avoided, I replied: 'I am afraid that I cannot agree to the plea of the Netherlands Minister. Of course, procedure is very important, but do not let us regard procedure like a stone goddess, immovable, relentless and completely strangling any real action. Procedure is made for men, and not men for procedure, and—in this particular case—the time factor is extremely important. I think, therefore, that I have no choice but to insist that this proposal of mine should be discussed by the Committee now.'

The atmosphere round the table was now very heated. To Plymouth's assistance came the Swedish representative Baron Palmstierna and the Polish representative Count E. Raczyński. They seized firmly on procedural obstacles and did their best, helped by Corbin, to bury beneath these the reality of the Portuguese question. All Plymouth had to do was pick up the apples as they fell at his feet.

In the final event the Portuguese question was postponed until the next plenary session, and the Committee settled down to composing the communiqué about the present day's work. This proved to be far from easy. Passions were roused, arguments raged, demands multiplied. Each side was anxious that its point of view should be especially clearly reflected in the communiqué. Everyone who had spoken during the meeting was concerned to see that the sense of his words was correctly given. It took about two hours before the final text was agreed, but, in contrast to the communiqués on previous meetings, this document reflected pretty accurately what had actually taken place.

It was after nine o'clock when I, accompanied by S. B. Kagan, came out into the street from the Foreign Office. A fine drizzle was falling, low clouds drove across the sky. Kagan remarked: 'We've been sitting there five hours without a break, and nobody even offered us a cup of tea at tea-time! It's not like the English at all.'

'Yes,' I agreed, 'passions in the Committee are rising so high that even the age-old English traditions can't stand the strain. . . . It all looks as though we're in for a hectic time. . . .'

And that hypothesis was duly confirmed as time passed.

The open posing of the question of the Fascist powers' violation of the Agreement on Non-intervention was an undoubted step forward in comparison with the diplomatic spillikins with which the Committee had occupied itself during the first few weeks of its existence. This was due entirely to the efforts of the Soviet side.

But we recognised quite clearly that now the Fascist powers would rush to counter-attack us. And this did in fact happen in the second half of October. One after another came the Notes from Germany, Italy and Portugal, advancing accusations against the U.S.S.R. as a state supplying arms to the Spanish Republic.

Seven plenary sessions of the Committee were devoted to the consideration of the complaints from both sides.[1]

And from the beginning Plymouth as Chairman established the following procedure: a complaint received by the Committee was passed on to the government against which it was directed, with a request that it should furnish an explanation; and

1. I mean the meetings which took place on 7, 9, 23 and 28 October and 4 and 12 November. On one of these days, 4 November to be precise, there were two sessions—one in the morning and one in the afternoon.

when such explanation was forthcoming, it and the complaint together were considered at a plenary meeting. As a rule the governments accused of violating the Agreement on Non-intervention completely denied their guilt, and as a result the Committee was put in an extremely difficult position. It had no means of its own for checking the truth or falsehood of accusations, and the 'facts' alleged by the two sides were diametrically opposed. In the end Lord Plymouth would declare that the accusation was unproven, and proceed to the next item on the agenda. In the course of the debate, however, passions would run high, the opposing sides would refuse to give way, and all this had wide repercussions far beyond the Committee itself.

A fine little specimen of how the discussion of a complaint would go in the Committee is provided by the meeting on 23 October, which I have described in detail above. Even more lively was the following meeting, on 28 October, when discussion was concluded on the complaints of violation of non-intervention by Germany, Italy and Portugal. Naturally I was once again alone against them all, and not because all 26 representatives of the capitalist countries really found the replies of Germany, Italy and Portugal satisfactory. Not at all! The Swedish Ambassador Palmstierna, who sat on my left, more than once in the course of the discussion made *sotto voce* such remarks as 'Disgusting!' 'Disgraceful!' 'There are no limits to their impudence!'—referring to the representatives of the Fascist powers. And the Czech envoy, Jan Masaryk, speaking to me after the meeting was over, used even stronger expressions in his estimate of the position of Germany and Italy. There were other members of the Committee (for instance the Norwegian Colban, the Greek Simopoulos, and some others) who were deeply shocked by the unceremonious lying of Grandi and Bismarck. But in the meetings they all remained obstinately silent, keeping their eyes on the green cloth of the table, and by so doing they assisted the Fascists' evil cause. They were all petrified with fear of the 'Great Powers', of Nazi Germany in the first place.

Taking advantage of this, Lord Plymouth did his best to under-line my isolation. Repeatedly he would speak immediately after I had spoken, expressing the diametrically opposite view, and then enquire of all those present: 'May I take it that the rest of the Committee's members share my opinion?'

'The rest' would say nothing, and Plymouth would take this as the expression of complete agreement. Of course, in such cases the Committee could not take any final decision, since the unanimity principle operated. None the less, Plymouth's manœuvres were undoubtedly of political significance; he was as it were demonstrating for the benefit of world public opinion that all Europe was united in a single opinion, you see, and only those intolerable Bolsheviks were stirring things up.

That was how it was when Italy's reply to the accusation of violating non-intervention was being assessed. The same thing happened when our complaint of 24 October against Portugal came up for discussion.

On the second of these occasions a parallel complaint to ours had been published by the government of the Spanish Republic. Monteiro, the Portuguese Minister for Foreign Affairs, had to produce explanations for the Committee on both these com-plaints simultaneously. His reply was amazing, first of all on account of its size: 21 pages of typescript for the u.s.s.r. and 46 for the Spanish Republic, or 67 sheets all told! I had every justification for my ironic comment that Monteiro deserved high marks for diligence, which was no doubt to be explained by his desire to make the most of the chance, rare for Portugal, of cut-ting a dash on the international stage.

But even more amazing was the content of Monteiro's com-positions. In them he began by attempting, feebly and un-convincingly enough, to rebut the factual accusations against Portugal of infringement of the Agreement on Non-intervention; but then he went on to counter-accusation. And there, swept away by a surge of inspiration, he came out with any number of the most patent absurdities.

Monteiro accused the u.s.s.r. of aiming at 'European domination', for which purpose Moscow was supposed to want to turn Spain into a 'Communist republic', but principally to 'fall upon Portugal'. Then came the allegation that in March 1936 Soviet vessels had brought 'large quantities of arms' to Spain, also 'chemical products for the poisoning of food and water'. There was also mention of the new Soviet Ambassador, appointed in the autumn of that year, having arrived in Madrid accompanied by an entourage of 140 persons, backed up by 100 aeroplanes, with a fantastic number of pilots and military experts. Such 'revelations' ornamented almost every page of the Portuguese reply. I held it up to cruel ridicule in my speech, and compared Monteiro to a tragic actor from the provinces, playing an old melodrama refurbished with modern trappings, and trying to scare his audience to death with his rendering of the 'Communist devil, complete with horns and tail'.

I said: '. . . Of course the sympathy of the peoples of the u.s.s.r. is on the side of democracy in Spain, and we have no reason to apologise for this; but this is not the main motive actuating Soviet foreign policy. The Soviet Government considers that at the present time in Spain there is going on a great advance battle between the forces of peace and the forces of war. The Spanish Government represents the forces of peace, and the Rebel Generals represent the forces of war.

'If the Spanish Government eventually succeeds in the suppression of rebellion it will not only retain one more Power on the side of peace, but it will also profoundly influence the whole situation in Europe, by inspiring new confidence in democracy and in the peaceful settlement of international questions. In this event the danger of war, which today looms so dark on the horizon, would be greatly lessened and the political sky of Europe be cleared of many of its present clouds.

'But if, on the contrary, success goes to the Rebel Generals, supported in contravention of the Non-intervention Agreement by certain Powers, then not only Spain will suffer internal disaster, but the outlook in Europe will be blackened to the last degree, because the victory of the rebels would mean such a tremendous encouragement to all the forces of aggression and hatred and destruction in Europe that terrible military catastrophe would engulf our part of the world in the very near future.

'That is the main reason why the Soviet Government and the peoples of the Soviet Union have so taken to heart the present trouble in Spain. The constant policy of international peace pursued by the Soviet Union inspires the present attitude of the Soviet Union towards Spanish affairs.'

This was a very necessary explanation at that time, for the fairy tales of the Soviet Union's desire to create a 'Communist republic' in Spain were widely current in Europe, and not in the Fascist countries alone; many politicians believed them in the u.s.a. and in Britain and France. The firm declaration by the Soviet side in the Committee (repeated more than once thereafter) that the actions of the u.s.s.r. on the 'Spanish question' were ruled by considerations of the peace and security of the nations of Europe, put a keen weapon with which to fight Fascist aggression into the hands of democrats the world over.

And how did the other members of the Committee react to our statement at the meeting of 28 October? Grandi and Bismarck, of course, did all they could to support Portugal, and the others as usual said nothing, modestly casting down their eyes. How did Plymouth behave? Plymouth for his part did everything possible to whitewash Portugal and to show how unaccommodating and stiff-necked those Bolsheviks were.

It was clear that no good was to be looked for from the Committee. Therefore the Soviet government had instructed me to make public at that same meeting, on 28 October, a new statement from our side, which said:

'The proceedings of the Committee have convinced the Soviet Government that at present there are no guarantees against further supply to the Rebel Generals of war materials. In these circumstances the Soviet Government is of the opinion that until such guarantees are created and an effective control over the strict fulfilment of the obligations regarding non-intervention established, those Governments who consider supplying the legitimate Spanish Government as conforming to international law, international order and international justice are morally entitled not to consider themselves more bound by the Agreement than those Governments who supply the rebels in contravention of the Agreement.'

This statement, the third within a month, by the Soviet government, affirmed even more definitely than the two preceding ones (of 7 and 23 October) that we would not let the baby be thrown out with the bath-water and ourselves be bound by the legal cobweb of non-intervention, disregarded by the Fascist powers. In the existing situation justice and political horse-sense demanded that we should supply the Spanish democrats with arms.

Looking back now on the events of those years, one sees more clearly than ever how correct the position of our government was. If anything is to be regretted, it is only that the geographical distance of Spain from the u.s.s.r. and the balance of world power then obtaining prevented us from rendering even more effective aid to the Spanish Republic.

In connection with the meeting of the Committee on 28 October, one half-comic episode remains in my mind. It (the meeting) began at 3 p.m. When the clock struck five, I remembered that at the last meeting our hosts had not bothered to regale the Committee's members with the traditional cup of five o'clock tea. I thought to myself: 'Well, if the Plymouths and Corbins are going to make us sit at this table and listen to quantities of hypocritical-diplomatical nonsense, at least let them provide us with tea and sandwiches!'

And so, in the midst of a fierce tussle over infringement by Italy of the Agreement on Non-intervention, I assumed my most innocent expression, suddenly turned to Plymouth and said: 'On a point of order, Mr. Chairman . . .'

Plymouth looked at me, puzzled and suspicious. He might have been waiting for me to throw a bomb down on the table. His secretaries were also thrown into alarm; they were clearly having visions of some new and cunning moves by the Soviet side. Silence descended on the green-covered table. Everyone waited with bated breath to see what would happen.

'Yes, on a point of order,' I repeated, deliberately prolonging the moment of tension. '. . . may I suggest that we have a break now for a cup of tea?'

A sigh of relief went up round the hall. But now Plymouth and his secretaries found themselves excessively embarrassed. It appeared that no preparations had been made. There was a hurried consultation between the Chairman and his aides, and then Plymouth announced with dignity, as a lord should: 'I am informed that there will be tea and refreshments provided at 6.30, when we will adjourn for a short time.'

From that day forth tea and sandwiches were served to the Committee at five o'clock without any further reminder being needed. The precedent had been created, and from then on the almighty (in England) power of tradition took over.

6

Bad miscalculations of
Bismarck and Grandi

Stormy though the meetings of 23 and 28 October were, the temperature of the political passions aroused reached its peak only at the plenary meeting of 4 November. This was the day when the complaints of Germany, Italy and Portugal of violation of the Agreement on Non-intervention by the u.s.s.r. were to be discussed.

Each of the three Fascist powers had sent a special Note to the Committee accusing the Soviet Union of violating the aforesaid Agreement. Each of the Fascist powers had taken the greatest pains to make it look as though its protest was based on information acquired by it independently and totally unconnected with the sources of the other two states friendly to it. They thought this would look more convincing for the Committee's members. But this game of the Fascist triumvirate was very quickly exposed and brought to nothing by the Soviet side. We had been immediately struck by the almost complete coincidence of a whole series of the accusations against the u.s.s.r., even of their actual wording, especially as between the German and Italian Notes. At the afternoon session I said straight out: '. . . study of the German, Italian and Portuguese Notes and also the circumstances of their presentation, leaves one under the impression that the spiritual father of these allegations against the Soviet Government is the Italian Representative, and the other two Governments have freely borrowed from his not too reliable sources'.

Bismarck and Calheiros tried to deny, quite baldly, the truth of my accusation, but when I repeated my conjecture at the next meeting, on 12 November, Grandi, who was not remarkable for his restraint or caution, exclaimed with almost schoolboy cheek: 'I am very proud of my sons!'

Not that there was actually much to be proud of. The accusations put forward against the U.S.S.R. were distinguished by their vagueness. Even Lord Plymouth, who was far from being sympathetic to the U.S.S.R., was shocked by the feebleness of the case presented by the Fascists and said directly that 'I do not see sufficiently precise evidence or facts to enable us to consider that an infringement of the Agreement has been proved'.

A vivid example of the frivolity with which the Fascist powers' Notes had been composed is provided by the bitter argument about the two Soviet ships *Neva* and *Kuban* that took place at the two meetings of 4 and 12 November. This argument had its prehistory.

From the very beginning of the Spanish conflict the broad masses of the Soviet people took their stand firmly and decidedly on the side of Spanish democracy. As early as 5 August an enormous public meeting of support for the Spanish Republic had taken place in Red Square in Moscow, under the chairmanship of N. M. Shvernik, head of the All-Union Council of Trade Unions; after that the women workers of the *Tryokhgorka*[1] addressed an ardent appeal to all members of the Soviet trade unions to start collecting money to aid Spanish women and children. The money flooded in, and amounted to a very large sum in a short space of time. This was used to buy food and clothing. These gifts for Spain were then loaded on board the vessels *Neva* and *Kuban*, which in late September and early October safely delivered their cargo to the Spanish port of Alicante.

And here in the German Note of complaint appeared the following points:

1. Familiar form of the name of a famous textile factory—Translator's note.

E

'Accusation 6. On 25 September the Russian steamship *Neva* called at the port of Alicante. She had on board provisions, skins, arms and ammunition, which were declared as provisions. Moreover 12 Russian pilots were on the steamer and they proceeded to Madrid.

'Accusation 7. The steamship *Kuban* under the Russian flag called at the same port on 4 October with provisions and ammunition.'

Regarding this, Plymouth remarked: 'The loading in the Soviet ports, and the unloading in the Spanish ports was witnessed by thousands of people and in the Spanish port they anchored in the midst of foreign men-of-war, including German and Italian; and the unloading proceeded in broad daylight. In such circumstances it would be inconceivable that any "clandestine" unloading of munitions could take place without a single person noticing such munitions. The German as well as the Italian "allegations", however, did not give a single instance of such testimony.'

Bismarck attempted to allay Plymouth's doubts. He declared that there were statements by witnesses, but the witnesses could not be named as their lives might be endangered.

Grandi supported his German colleague, saying that the commander and officers of the Italian cruiser *Verazzano*, which had been in Alicante at the time, fully confirmed that arms and ammunition had been unloaded from the *Neva* and the *Kuban*.

I laughed Bismarck's and Grandi's arguments to scorn, and clearly succeeded in destroying their hearers' faith in their words. Then Grandi put about on another tack and plunged into argument on naval technology. The essential point was that the *Neva* and *Kuban* had been sitting very low in the water when they docked, below the Plimsoll line, so that such a draught could not have been induced by a cargo of food and consumer goods, and that there must therefore have been guns, tanks and machine-guns underneath the food and clothing. I protested firmly against Grandi's allegations, and not only protested, but quoted precise figures and calculations showing the total lack of foundation for the Italian Ambassador's accusations. The latter's technological argumentation, however, made a certain impression on some members of the Committee (obviously because they had little understanding of the subject), and the Swede Palmstierna and the Pole Raczyński began talking of the need to study all this more fully. Plymouth also began to waver.

Taking advantage of the momentary confusion, Bismarck and Grandi proposed that the discussion of the Fascist complaints against the U.S.S.R. be postponed. They sensed that they were going down. They needed to gather together some new, more convincing proof that the Soviet Union had infringed the Agreement on Non-intervention, and to do that they needed time.

I spoke firmly against all postponements and reproached the Committee with making its work resemble a film played in slow motion. After a long, fierce argument I at last succeeded in shaking the members' faith in Grandi's intricacies of maritime practice. When the Committee settled down to drawing up its communiqué, and Francis Hemming wanted to include in the text Palmstierna's remark about the need to check the real cause of the Soviet ships having been so low in the water, the Swedish Ambassador himself flatly refused to have it in. Clearly he was embarrassed by the prospect of appearing before world opinion as an ally of Bismarck and Grandi.

The Soviet side succeeded in giving entirely satisfactory explanations on all the other counts of the Fascist complaint also, to the extent that Plymouth had at last to declare the complaints unproven.

The Fascist attack against the U.S.S.R. had ended in complete fiasco.

On the same day, 4 November, two more incidents took place in the Committee's meetings which were extremely disadvantageous to Germany, Italy and Portugal.

The first was as follows. Answering my assurances that the *Neva* and the *Kuban* took to Spain only food and clothing for Spanish women and children, Grandi declared, with a cynicism hard to convey to the reader: 'Every time that an appeal is made to the public opinion of civilised countries by those who, for one reason or another, are interested in distorting truth, this appeal is always made in the name of women and children. If a Power is engaged in a colonial operation, one immediately hears of massacres of native women and children. If the aircraft of the Spanish Nationalists carry out war operations, it is straightaway said that the harmless women and children of democratic Spain are the only victims of such operations. If Soviet Russia starts subscriptions and sends goods to Spain, these funds and these goods are sent to the women and children of Spain. On reading the Soviet statements one really wonders whether the Spanish civil war is not after all a strife between the men under General Franco and the women and children that Soviet Russia has taken under her motherly wing. . . .'

This speech was definitely a tactical error on Grandi's part. Everyone instantly became as it were on his guard. A tense silence settled over the hall. Some of the members of the Committee shrugged their shoulders and exchanged glances.

My neighbour the Swedish Ambassador Palmstierna exclaimed: 'Disgusting!' under his breath. Many heard his exclamation and nodded their heads in sympathy. But Grandi's Italian temperament had carried him away to such an extent that he noticed nothing, and went on with his tirade against women and children.

Speaking in reply to the Italian Ambassador the same day after lunch, I began my speech thus:

'I am not at all surprised to hear him [the Italian representative —translator] say such strong words against purely humanitarian feelings and humanitarian work. He even ridiculed the bombing of women and children in Madrid . . . and perhaps I misunderstood him, but he made me think he is a bitter enemy of the female sex and of children, and completely indifferent to the sufferings and anguish which these women and children are enduring in Spain at the present time. I am not surprised by all that because it is a part of the creed that he represents, that creed which means war and war of the most brutal, naked and abhorrent kind. It is not the first time that from his country we hear war glorified, or witness a complete and utter disregard of human suffering and human life.

'In this respect the Soviet Government and the Soviet peoples are in direct opposition to the views of the Italian representative. The Soviet Union stands for peace, for peaceful constructive work, for the creation of a happy and prosperous life, for the mitigation and eventual abolition of all the horrors which humanity is subject to today. Just because of this the Soviet Union has always pursued and still pursues a policy of peace, disarmament and the principles of the Covenant of the League of Nations. This does not mean that the Soviet Union will not fight in defence of her own territory; of course she will fight hard for it, and, moreover, she is adequately prepared for such a fight. But we do not glorify war; we understand that war is a great calamity, and that the horrors and sufferings of war must be mitigated as far as possible.'

My speech had its effect on the majority of the Committee's members. Palmstierna shook my hand, . . . but he did so under the table, so that nobody could see the gesture. One felt that some members of the Committee, in spite of the gulf dividing us on many questions, were ready to follow the Swedish Ambassador's example . . .

The second incident of 4 November was of a rather different nature. At this time the situation at the Spanish front had assumed a very threatening character. General Mola was immobilised at the Guadarrama, as before, but the southern column of Fascist forces, headed by Franco, was moving irresistibly towards Madrid, and on 3 November was only 15 kilometres away from the capital. That day a council of the military and civil leaders of the rebellion was held in Avila, at which it was decided that the entry of the Franco forces into Madrid must take place on 7 November. The rebels worked out a detailed programme of this, for them, triumphal occasion. This provided for the departure from Valladolid of a somewhat cumbrous official *cortège*: 20 lorries full of Falangist 'young ladies' who as soon as 'order' was restored in the capital were to hand out coffee and buns to the 'fifth column'; then 11 bands; after them, the Fascist Mayor of Madrid (appointed by Franco) with his Councillors, the Civil Governor, the Director-General of security, agents, policemen, secret police. After all these, several hours later, Franco himself was to leave his headquarters, accompanied by his general staff and by German and Italian representatives.

The rebels even picked the *venue* for a military parade in Madrid; a speech by Franco suitable to the occasion was prepared. The white horse on which the dictator was to ride into the capital was already in its stable at Alcorcon.[1] Even a thanksgiving service in Madrid Cathedral was ordered. Everything, in fact, positively everything, was prepared by the rebels for their triumphal entry into Madrid.

This atmosphere, this expectation of triumph close at hand for the Spanish Fascists (and for Hitler and Mussolini also) had an inebriating effect upon Grandi. And at the close of the meeting on 4 November his Italian temperament once again did him a bad turn.

About six o'clock I noticed one of the secretaries of the Italian Embassy hurriedly enter with a sheaf of paper, and start to squeeze his way through to his chief. A minute later Grandi asked to speak, and, waving the bits of paper just received from the secretary, proclaimed triumphantly:

'. . . I cannot, however, refrain from reading to the Committee a telegram which has only reached me during the sitting of the Committee. It comes from Rome, and my Government has received it from Spain and from a very reliable source. The Soviet Representative during the discussion today has many times and repeatedly declared that no Soviet aeroplanes are fighting under the red flag of Spanish Communists. I am able to contradict that assertion in the most emphatic way. The telegram

1. A small place near Madrid.

which reached me just now reads: "The Nationalist Spanish
Forces have captured four tanks of Soviet origin; one Russian
bomber was brought down yesterday, 3 November, with a crew
of 3 Soviet subjects; and 4 November," that is, today, "the
Spanish Nationalist forces have captured 2 more Russian war-
planes, manned by Soviet pilots. Of these pilots one is wounded,
the other unhurt".'

'I think that all of us are grateful that the Italian representative
has such fresh news from the front,' I remarked ironically.

Grandi was not slow to respond: 'Yes, news from the front
where your friends are being beaten.'

'*Rira bien qui rira le dernier*,' I retorted sharply. 'But I should
like to stress this: The Italian representative astounds us with
some very sensational news—some up-to-the-minute information
from General Franco, via Rome—of what is happening in
Spain. Does not the very fact that he is in receipt of such stop-
press news prove conclusively the very close and intimate relations
existing between the Italian Government and the rebels? As to
the authenticity of his news—well! that is another matter, but
I am very much afraid it may prove no more reliable than the
reports, from the same source, which I exposed just now.'

It did not escape my notice that then, at the 4 November
meeting, my exclaiming '*Rira bien qui rira le dernier*' seemed to
many members of the Committee to be merely putting the best
face possible on a bad case. Some even smiled ironically. But by
the following plenary meeting, on 12 November, when all the
'ends' left over from the consideration of complaints were
tidied up, the feeling in the Committee had changed considerably.

The so pompously publicised Fascist advance on Madrid on 7
November had failed completely. At the very last moment the
heroic defenders of the Republic, supported by two International
Brigades, halted the Fascists on the threshold of the capital.
Now the ironical smiles were in Grandi's direction, and a little
later they were replaced by open ridicule of his boasting . . .

The meeting that took place on 4 November is involuntarily
associated in my mind with the name of Winston Churchill.

After Hitler came to power this fierce enemy of Communism
and of the Soviet state began to realign his bearings. He immediately sensed danger to the British Empire from German
Nazism. Being much cleverer than Neville Chamberlain and
Halifax, Churchill did not believe in the possibility of meeting
this danger by setting Germany against the u.s.s.r. Once in
conversation with me he said: 'Neville's a fool . . . He thinks he
can ride the tiger.'

That was why Churchill after 1933 became a supporter of the
'renaissance of the Entente of the First World War', that is, of a
military alliance of Britain, France and the u.s.s.r. Of course, it
caused him to wince that the third member of this alliance must
now be a Socialist state, not Tsarist Russia, but for the salvation
of the British Empire he was prepared to swallow even this
bitter pill. In the middle of 1934 Churchill on his own initiative
made my acquaintance, and thereafter made every effort to
develop our relations. On 5 November, the day after the meeting
of the Committee which I have described above, I had lunch
with him, and we talked at length of current political problems,
of the importance of a united front of Britain, France and the
u.s.s.r. against the danger of German aggression. Then the talk
passed to events in Spain. On this question our opinions differed
sharply. Churchill was an opponent of the Spanish Republic and
openly sympathised with Franco. We argued for a long time and
even got quite worked up. In the end Churchill said: 'It's not
worth while worrying one another . . . We need all the unity we
can get on the main, the fundamental question. . . . Hitler is
equally dangerous to you and to us. . . .'

Churchill drew on his cigar, and then, blowing out a great
cloud of smoke, added conciliatorily: 'Anyway, why argue. . . .
A week will pass, and all this unpleasant Spanish business will
disappear from the scene. . . . Have you seen today's newspaper
reports? . . . Another day or two and Franco will be in Madrid,
and who will remember the Spanish Republic then?'

I laughed and said: 'In the history of our civil war, Mr.
Churchill, there were moments when many people thought that

all was lost for the Bolsheviks . . . Yet today I have the honour
of talking with you in the capacity of Ambassador of the Union
of Soviet Socialist Republics!'

Churchill shook his head and murmured something about
there being a great deal of difference between Russia and Spain.
. . . It was clear that his estimate of the prospects of the struggle
in Spain were very similar to those of Grandi. . . .

Let us return, however, to the Committee for 'Non-intervention'. Summing up the results of my first month's work on
it, I had no reason to feel dissatisfied. The Soviet side, in spite
of extremely unfavourable conditions (for, after all, the u.s.s.r.
was in effect alone against 26 states) had succeeded in tearing the
mask from this hypocritical invention of the capitalist powers
and exposing their conspiracy against the Spanish Republic. And
this was of very great importance in mobilising world opinion
on behalf of Spanish democracy! The Soviet side had also
succeeded in showing that the interest of the u.s.s.r. in events in
Spain flowed not from nationalistic or egoistic calculations, but
was dictated solely by concern for peace throughout the world.
Lastly, the Soviet side had succeeded by its statements of 7, 23
and 28 October in demonstrating to the world that the u.s.s.r.
would never be a party to the strangling of Spanish democracy,
but would, on the contrary, give it all possible aid. And this
firm word of our government was straightaway confirmed by
concrete action.

Here, I think, one should clear up once and for all the question
of whether the real position of the Soviet government in August
1936 was in any way different from that to which we came in
October of the same year. This can be settled in few words.

When on 25 August our government signed the Agreement
on Non-intervention it quite sincerely proposed to observe this
strictly, but on condition, of course, that obligations under it
were equally strictly observed by other powers (Germany and
Italy first of all).

The correctness of this stand was in no way in doubt, since

we were unshakably convinced that if intervention from outside was excluded the Spaniards would be able to settle their internal difference without the cause of peace and democracy suffering loss. September was seen by us as the time of trial, and in the course of that month neither arms nor ammunition were sent from the u.s.s.r. to Spain. The shouting of the Fascist powers about Soviet aeroplanes and tanks operating in Spain in September and October 1936 had no foundation in fact. But when September passed by and Germany and Italy were continuing, with Britain and France standing passively by, to supply Franco with arms and 'advisers' in ever-increasing quantities, the u.s.s.r. was compelled to change its original intention.

In October it was decided to aid Spain by the supply of arms, and the statement we made in the Committee on 7 October was a signal for all those who had signed the Agreement that the Soviet government did not propose to play the part of a simpleton, used as an instrument by others to carry out a foul deed. And it was only in the days of the Fascist advance on the capital of Spain (i.e. about 7–10 November) that the first Soviet tanks and aeroplanes were tried in battle before Madrid.

When Grandi at the meeting of 4 November read his telegram about the capture by Franco forces of 'Russian bombers' it was a complete lie. Not a single Soviet plane had yet taken off into the Spanish sky. And as for 'Russian bombers', there was no question of any such thing. The first contingents of Soviet planes sent to Spain consisted entirely of fighters. Soviet bombers did not make their appearance till much later.

7

The main *dramatis personae*

BEFORE proceeding to illumine the further history of the Committee for 'Non-intervention', I should like to pause in order to describe some of the persons playing a major part in it. Such were the nine men who made up what was known as 'the Chairman's Sub-committee'. As I have already related, this Sub-committee gradually, step by step, substituted itself for the plenary meeting of the Committee, and in the end concentrated in its own hands the entire functioning of the Committee. A clear idea of the members of the 'Big Nine' will make it easier for the reader to understand all that will be spoken of later.

I shall start with Lord Plymouth. He was an aristocrat born and bred, whose family had received a barony in the early 16th century. He was the fifteenth Baron Windsor, and married the daughter of the eleventh Earl of Wemyss.

After going to the aristocratic school at Eton and then to Cambridge University, Plymouth went into politics, as befitted a Conservative by birthright and one of the largest landowners in the country (he owned 12,000 hectares of land); he was a member of the London County Council, a Member of Parliament, Parliamentary Under-secretary in various Ministries and, in 1939, Under-secretary of state at the Foreign Office.

Tall, broad-shouldered, fair, about fifty years old, with a large head covered with faded-yellow hair, with a calmly respectable expression of face, Plymouth was, as it were, the incarnation of all customarily associated with the word 'lord'. He had beautiful manners and a turn of speech of diplomatic refinement. All his movements, gestures and idiosyncrasies were informed by a worthy solemnity. In addition, Plymouth was remarkable for his great restraint: in all the two and a half years of the Committee's work I cannot recall a single instance of him losing his temper and speaking rudely to anyone (though he had plenty of occasion to do so).

However, in this large, imposing and well-groomed body dwelt a small, slow-moving and timid mind. Nature and education had made Plymouth a practically ideal personification of English political mediocrity, nourished by the traditions of the past and by well-worn sentiments.

As Chairman of the Committee Plymouth presented an entirely helpless and often comic figure. True, he could assume a serious and impartial air and sum up in smooth phrases the discussion that had taken place (his long parliamentary experience told here), and he would undoubtedly have made a good leader of some good, solid, quiet commission investigating the question of where a new university should be opened or where the boundary line between two counties ought to run. But the Committee for 'Non-intervention' in Spanish Affairs was not a bit like such a commission. It was not a sleepy backwater, but a stream rushing headlong over stones. Danger lurked at every step. Unexpected moves and counter-moves every now and then created critical situations. Even in the League of Nations—that first-born child of the new, democratised diplomacy—there was nothing like this.

The Chairman of the Committee had to face at almost every meeting the explosion of political depth-charges, the force of real diplomatic storms. He was called on to display quickness, percipience and flexibility of thought, the ability to propose a compromise acceptable to both sides. And Plymouth had not got all this. It is not surprising that he often got himself into a most difficult position, and then . . . Perhaps the best thing will be to sketch in a typical incident.

On the agenda for the day there is some thorny question. A

fierce debate flares up. The opinions of the Soviet and the Fascist representatives are directly opposed. The representatives of the so-called 'democratic' powers are wavering. Plymouth as Chairman should take up a definite stand and win over a majority of the Committee's members to it. But Plymouth does not know what to settle on. His face expresses agonised bewilderment. He turns to his advisers—Francis Hemming, who used to sit on his left, and Roberts, on his right. A hurried consultation in whispers begins among them. The recommendations of the advisers turn out to be at variance, often diametrically opposed, for, as I have already mentioned, Hemming sympathised with the Spanish democrats and Roberts was a supporter of Franco. The indecision on Plymouth's countenance grows greater, he goes red and then pale, and last, assuming his severely impartial air, proclaims solemnly: 'The meeting is adjourned!'

This was Plymouth's usual gambit in all difficult moments. Can one wonder that the Committee and the Sub-committee throughout the whole of the time of their existence often resembled a ship without a captain?

A different type of man altogether was the representative of France, Charles Corbin. A Catholic by conviction, a lawyer by education, and a professional diplomat by working experience, by the age of sixty he had seen diplomacy in practice, in Paris, Madrid, Rome and Brussels, and since 1933 had occupied the high post of French Ambassador in London. There were rumours that he had been through a bitter personal drama, after which he remained a bachelor for ever.

In appearance Corbin bore little resemblance to the typical Frenchman. With his greying, once brown hair, smooth-shaven face and calm, steely-grey eyes he was more reminiscent of a descendant of the Vikings. Corbin's movements were unhurried and confident, he spoke in a rather flat, even voice with small coughs and throat-clearings, his emotions were firmly locked away inside the diplomatic casing. Never, even in moments of extreme provocation, did he raise his voice or forget the rules of good behaviour. Corbin usually spoke in French at the Committee's meetings, although he could speak English fluently. He always lined up with Plymouth (which entirely accorded with the positions of France and Britain on the Spanish question), but his line was clearer and more consistent than that of the Chairman. Corbin considered the Spanish war an irritating complication for France, and if it could not be got rid of then at least it must be damped down so far as was possible, and every conceivable measure taken to bring military action to a speedy end. Whether the end result was victory for democracy or victory for Fascism, or some compromise between the two, was of secondary importance. His only concern was that events in Spain should cease to confuse the diplomatic cards for Paris.

The French Ambassador belonged to that school of Western diplomats, numerous in the thirties, who rejected any large, far-seeing (even if still bourgeois) conception of politics and became completely bogged down in the mud of petty, day-to-day political scrabbling. That was the kind of line Corbin pursued the whole time, one meeting after another, in the discussion of every concrete question that came up before the Committee or the Sub-committee. Now, in the light of history, it becomes particularly clear that Corbin, as the representative of France, bears just as heavy a responsibility as Plymouth for the short-sighted, shameful line of conduct pursued then by the 'democratic' powers towards the Spanish Republic.

A very colourful figure was that of Belgium's representative, Baron Cartier de Marchienne. He was a typical 'diplomat of the old school'. He was well over sixty, his head crowned with thick grey hair. Cartier was seen at his most striking at big official receptions. In full-dress uniform, a ribbon across his shoulder, with his luxuriant grey whiskers and his monocle he looked as if he had come straight out of a 19th-century picture of 'a foreign Ambassador'.

Cartier had a rich American wife, a coarse and vulgar woman who in conversation with other diplomatic ladies did not hesitate to proclaim: 'I would never have married my Cartier if he hadn't been a Baron.'

Cartier had the reputation of a good-natured and courteous man. He was always ready to help the needy (regardless of whether these were represented by an individual or a whole country), but only so long as this did not mean any difficulty for himself. If on the other hand obstacles of any sort arose, Cartier did not even try to overcome them, but simply spread out his hands in a helpless gesture, as if to say: 'I should be glad to do something, but see for yourself—it's impossible.'

Cartier's head was completely empty. Of course good manners and long diplomatic training enabled him to conceal this to some extent, under ordinary circumstances. But when the Belgian Ambassador had to come into contact with really serious problems, his true face at once became apparent.

So it was with the Committee for 'Non-intervention'. It must be said straight out—he did not like it. Not because the Baron sympathised with the Spanish democrats—oh, no! The Belgian Ambassador had very much more sympathy with Franco. Cartier disliked the Committee for entirely different reasons; participation in the work of this body was so unlike the methods, dear to his heart, of the old diplomacy. In it one was so often called upon to take up a quite definite attitude on a disputed issue, and in broad daylight too, under the eyes of world opinion! Cartier's whole nature and training protested against it. But by force of circumstance Cartier was none the less obliged to sit at the Committee table, and even to be on the Chairman's Sub-committee.

Actually he very soon found a very simple way out of this embarrassing situation: whatever debates might be in progress, Cartier silently doodled, drawing little devils on his notepad. Usually drowsiness very quickly overtook him at this occupation. The Baron would lean his head on his hand, start to snore gently through his nose. When it came to taking a vote, Roberts, who sat beside Cartier, would delicately touch his sleeve. The Belgian Ambassador would wake up, turn his head about in confusion, as if not quite sure where he was, and waving his hands awkwardly would exclaim: 'Please repeat that once more! I must get things clear in my mind! I cannot decide so fast!'

It always ended with Cartier voting the same way as Plymouth and Corbin.

Also remarkable in his way was Sweden's representative, Baron Erik Palmstierna. Short in stature, dark, lively in his movements and with black, wavy hair in which some threads of silver gleamed, he was more like a Frenchman or an Italian than a Scandinavian. His face was pleasing and thoughtful, but too nervous, and an odd light flickered in his eye.

In his youth the Swedish envoy had served in the navy and had belonged to the Social-Democratic Party. With the passage of years he began to 'moult' politically, and in the days when I knew him in London considered himself a man who 'sympathised with all that was progressive'. But socialism now seemed to him too narrow and dogmatic, unable to contain the full complexity and variety of life.

Once he invited me to lunch with him. We sat side by side at table and talked in a leisurely way on various subjects. Suddenly Palmstierna looked sideways at me and asked: 'You are an atheist, of course?'

'Yes, I am an atheist,' I replied, 'and always have been.'

'I used to be an atheist too,' confessed Palmstierna, 'but my life's experience has compelled me to change the views of my youth.'

At the time I did not attribute any great significance to this conversation, but could not help but remember it when at the end of 1937 an English newspaper came into my hands which carried an announcement of the publication of a book by the Swedish Ambassador. The book had a strange and intriguing title—*The Horizons of Immortality*. I bought the book and read it. And what did I find? It was a collection of detailed records of spiritualistic conversations between Palmstierna and 'messengers from the other world'. I must admit I was shaken, and had to look at my Swedish colleague in quite a new light. The thought even came to mind: 'That is it: the *facies Hippocratica* of bourgeois society . . .'

As I have noted before, at the Committee table Palmstierna was my neighbour, and during meetings we not infrequently exchanged opinions and remarks. His mood at that time was liberal anti-Fascist. The Swedish envoy was rendered particularly indignant by Ribbentrop, who from November 1936 onwards replaced Prince Bismarck on the Committee. The longer the inglorious tale of the Committee's doings proceeded, the stronger became Palmstierna's indignation.

'I never thought,' he would often say, 'that diplomacy could fall so low. Why, what goes on here is a complete farce, a fraud, sheer hypocrisy. I feel sick when I listen to Plymouth and Corbin, let alone Grandi and Ribbentrop . . . How horrible! How disgusting!'

However, when in answer to these lamentations I invited him to help me in the fight against the aggressors, he took fright and beat a retreat. True, behind the scenes the Swedish envoy did try to give me what support he could, and not only moral support either. Sometimes he assisted me in my work with useful information. But Palmstierna could not bring himself to come out openly on my side. In part this was the fault of the general attitude of the Swedish government on the Spanish question, which was that they did not wish to enter into conflict with Germany. But in part Palmstierna's own views were to blame; in spite of his disgust at the behaviour of the four Western powers he still could not quite 'take' the Spanish democrats. They seemed to him 'too red'. The result was that Palmstierna continually wavered, got muddled, rushed from side to side, unable to take a firm and consistent line in the Committee.

In 1938 Palmstierna retired, but did not return to Sweden; he stayed on in England, as the head of some Anglo-Swedish trading concern. In diplomatic circles in London there were smiles as the story of his retirement and its attendant circumstances went the rounds. In 1937 Palmstierna attained the age limit for Swedish diplomatic workers—60. Exceptions were often made for Ambassadors and envoys, though, and of course Palmstierna had every chance of remaining his country's

F

representative in London for several years more. But . . . it was in
1937 that his *Horizons of Immortality* came out, and the Swedish
Ministry of Foreign Affairs took fright. They were not frightened
of Sweden's prestige in the eyes of the world suffering from their
envoy's being one with the spirits—not that! Apprehensions of
that sort were alien to them. What caused disquiet in the Swedish
Foreign Ministry was something else. What, they thought, if
the 'messengers from the other side' converse with Palmstierna
on diplomatic themes? What if they give him instructions on
different political questions? And what if those instructions are
at variance with those he has received from the Swedish government on the same questions? To whose voice will Palmstierna
then choose to harken . . . ?

To avoid risk, they decided in Stockholm to apply the general
rule, and, sweetening the pill as much as possible, forced retirement upon their London envoy.

A man of quite another disposition was Czechoslovakia's
representative, Jan Masaryk, son of the famous Thomas Masaryk,
who played such a great part in the creation of the bourgeois
Czechoslovak state. A hefty man, with a large head set squarely
on, he seemed the personification of health and energy.

Masaryk had lived for a long time in the u.s.a., and this had
left its mark not only on his English, which had an American
twang, but on his whole character. Of course, he considered himself a good Czech patriot, but there was always a struggle going
on in his mind between two tendencies: reason told him,
especially during the years of the second world war, that Czechoslovakia's future lay in the East, in close friendship with the
u.s.s.r.; but heart and everyday habit drew him to the West—
to the u.s.a., to England, to France. Once Masaryk said to me:
'No, I'm not a Socialist! Socialism scares me off. But I'm against
any kind of reaction. You could best of all classify me as a
European radical, who believes in science and the progress of
humanity and wants to serve them, but in his own way . . . In
an individualistic way . . . Maybe even a bit anarchically . . .'

This inner dualism gnawed at Masaryk in London, and gnawed him later when he was back in his own country, and I think it was principally this which was at the bottom of his premature death.[1]

Participation in the Committee for 'Non-intervention' was a burden, a painful trial, to Masaryk. In his soul he felt ardent sympathy for the Spanish democrats, and on the quiet he gave me every assistance in the fight against the Fascists. Particularly valuable was the information he provided on the plans and intentions of the Fascist representatives, and sometimes of those of the English and French as well. Masaryk was an extremely well-informed diplomat and had good contacts in the most varied circles. But he too, like Palmstierna, could not bring himself to the point of coming out openly on my side, for his instructions from Prague prescribed the observance of the utmost caution with respect to Nazi Germany. So at the meetings of the Committee and Sub-committee Masaryk was usually gloomily silent, and when this was impossible he confined himself to a few words only, and those as a rule vague. Masaryk often felt embarrassed towards me, and once he tried to explain to me the essence of his position: 'I'm the little boy in short pants, who can't do anything. You [meaning the Great Powers—IM.] are the hulking great lads who can do anything. You are fighting among yourselves, and no one knows who's going to win. I have to look out that the big boys don't trample me underfoot . . . You must understand my position, Czechoslovakia's position . . .'

Of course I did understand, but it was not much help to either the U.S.S.R., the Spanish Republic or, in the last resort, to Czechoslovakia herself.

Plymouth, Corbin, Cartier, Palmstierna and Masaryk represented at the Sub-committee table the camp of the so-called 'democratic' powers, and with all their differences they were in

1. In 1948, while Minister of Foreign Affairs of Czechoslovakia, Masaryk committed suicide.

the main carrying through the same political line, that personified in living form by the Chairman.

But at the same table sat the representatives of the Fascist camp also. There were three of them—the Ambassadors in London of Italy, Germany and Portugal. Of the last, Count Monteiro, there is little to be said. There was nothing in him to indicate any particular character. He seemed to me far too 'streamlined' in both external appearance and inner nature, and he played a quite insignificant part in the Committee, as a mere appendage to the two 'big Fascists', Dino Grandi and Joachim Ribbentrop. These two 'big boys', however, are worth speaking of in rather more detail.

About Grandi, first.

If the Swedish Ambassador Palmstierna looked like an Italian, then the Italian Ambassador Grandi in appearance rather suggested a Russian or a Pole. He was a man of solid build, with dark brown hair combed straight back and a carefully trimmed pointed beard. Under thick brows sat unusually bright eyes, their expression strangely combining sparks of merriment with the unmoved calm of the cynic. His moustaches stressed his big, stubborn mouth.

The general impression was a clever and cunning man, with whom one must be on one's guard.

Grandi was one of the principal figures of Italian Fascism; he and Mussolini stood together at its cradle. In 1922 he took a part in the 'march on Rome', and when Mussolini became dictator Grandi occupied a number of responsible posts in the Fascist administration, rising to be Minister of Foreign Affairs. Invested with ministerial powers, he made a very successful visit to the U.S.A. on Italy's behalf, and appeared with no less success as his country's representative at the League of Nations.

In the early thirties the name of the 37-year-old Grandi was loud in men's ears. Many looked on him as Mussolini's probable 'heir'. Suddenly, though, 'the hand of fate' reached out for the prospering 'statesman'.

It is a known fact that Mussolini regarded every major

personage in his entourage with deep suspicion. He sensed a rival in Grandi, and struck a decisive blow at the latter before he should become too dangerous: in mid-1932 Grandi lost his ministerial post and was sent as Italian Ambassador to London. It was equivalent to 'honorary exile'. Grandi thought that soon he would be out of disgrace and would return to Italy. But it did not happen; he had to live seven whole years in England.

My relations with Grandi were of an involved and contradictory nature. As an individual he was undoubtedly interesting; he was witty, he was eloquent. Conversations with Grandi were something I always considered useful, for he was one of the best-informed foreign Ambassadors in London, and from him one could quite often learn the very latest political and diplomatic news. Furthermore Grandi, unlike many diplomats, was frank, almost demonstratively frank with colleagues!

During the first three years of my work in London we often met, and we had no small number of interesting discussions. This was made easy by the relations then existing between the u.s.s.r. and Italy; they were 'friendly', in the diplomatic sense.

But as from 1935 the situation began to change sharply; the gulf between the u.s.s.r. and Italy grew ever wider. First owing to Italy's attack on Ethiopia, then because of Italian aggression in Spain. This was reflected in my personal relations with Grandi.

During the winter of 1935–6, at the time of the Italo-Ethiopian war, there was still as yet no open breach between us. But since the beginning of the war in Spain we found ourselves in diametrically opposed camps, and this actually at the table of the Committee for 'Non-Intervention', where extremely bitter skirmishes between us became an everyday occurrence. Grandi defended his country's policy not as a matter of duty alone, but with genuine enthusiasm, to which he was inspired not so much by general political aims as by purely personal ones. He was clearly flattered by the fact that after being left unmentioned and ignored for so long his name was now to be seen in the newspapers again, heard over the radio. He was again in the centre of the world's attention! The Committee offered Grandi a platform for frequent and effective speech-making. And since Ribbentrop (the other Fascist whale) was far inferior to Grandi in brain, eloquence, guile and skill, the impression was in the last resort created that it was the Ambassador of Italy, not that of Germany, who was the leader of the Fascist camp in the Committee.

This spurred Grandi on still more, stimulated his energy and ingenuity. But often his Italian temperament did him a bad turn. I have already related how disastrously for himself—and only through the fault of his temperament—Grandi spoke at the plenary meeting on 4 November 1936. Later on, similar misjudgments were repeated more than once, and each time I did my best to utilise them as weapons against Fascism.

The Committee was a real find for Grandi. His prestige in Italy began to grow rapidly. In 1937 Mussolini found it expedient to honour his Ambassador in London with the title of Count, and in 1939 Grandi was at last recalled from England and made Minister of Justice. After that he became a member of the Grand Fascist Council. Even later, in 1943, he took an active part in the deposition of Mussolini. Grandi apparently understood that 'classical Fascism', as represented by the late dictator, was no longer possible, and tried to replace it by a somewhat moderated form of 'neo-Fascism', hoping in so doing that he would be able to play a leading role in party and state. But Grandi's calculations were wrong again. The Italian people wanted no more of Fascism, whether old or new type. The result was that my 'London colleague' and ideological opponent disappeared, like many others, from the political horizon. . . .

Ribbentrop was in many respects the exact opposite of Grandi. Since I sat for a whole year diagonally opposite the German Ambassador at the table of the Committee for 'Non-intervention', I had the opportunity of studying him at close quarters. And I must without mincing words say that this was a coarse, dull-witted maniac, with the outlook and manners of a Prussian N.C.O. It has always remained a mystery to me how Hitler could have made such a dolt his chief adviser on foreign affairs. Not that he deserved a better adviser. After all, the foreign policy of the Third Reich, in forming which the Fuehrer undoubtedly played the main role, was no glittering work of art. In cases where the mailed fist sufficed, it did well enough. But when 'arguments' of that sort proved ineffective, it unfailingly suffered defeat. How otherwise is one to explain the fact that Hitler's diplomacy failed to avert the alliance between America, the Soviet Union and Britain? How explain the fact that there was no simultaneous attack on the u.s.s.r. by Germany and Japan together, such as Berlin had dreamed of so ardently?

Joachim Ribbentrop, ex-commercial traveller in champagne, stepped into the post of German Ambassador in London over the dead body of von Hesch,[1] and once there displayed such a lack of understanding of England and the English, such a monumental absence of tact, such a fantastically exaggerated opinion of himself, that he soon became a laughing-stock in the British capital. Of course, Ribbentrop was invited to receptions, and others went to those which he gave. Certain circles even fawned on him (remember, he represented a mighty power!). But those same people who had just dined or drunk tea in the German Embassy exploded, as soon as they were outside it, into savage ridicule of their host, and told one another anecdotes about his stupidity and conceit.

Ribbentrop's misadventures began literally with the first day of his arrival in Britain. There is a firmly established diplomatic

1. In the autumn of 1932, on the eve of Hitler coming to power, a new German Ambassador to London was appointed—Leopold von Hesch. He was an old diplomat, a cultured liberal, Weimar style, who enjoyed great popularity in British political circles. So long as Hitler did not feel himself quite secure enough, he retained Hesch in his post in London. But in the spring of 1936 Hesch 'died suddenly', in his bath, under extremely mysterious circumstances. Since this drama took place within the walls of the German Embassy, the British authorities were unable to carry out a post-mortem examination or establish the cause of death. His body was taken to Germany and buried there. In those years there were persistent rumours that Ribbentrop was concerned in Hesch's death, because he wished at all costs to free the post of German Ambassador in London for himself.

rule which lays down that an Ambassador is not an Ambassador until he has handed over his letters of credit to the head of the state to which he is accredited; in particular, he may not make speeches or give interviews of a political nature. But Ribbentrop on alighting from the train which brought him from Dover to London held a press conference then and there on the station, in the course of which he criticised Britain for underestimating 'the Red Menace' and called on her to join with Germany in fighting Communism. In a country which makes a religion of traditions and customs handed down from one's ancestors, Ribbentrop's behaviour shocked even dyed-in-the-wool Conservatives.

The first shock was followed by others. At a Court reception, instead of greeting the English King with the customary hand-shake, Ribbentrop gave the Nazi salute. This really shook monarchical circles to their foundation.

He behaved in an equally absurd manner when making the visits to other Ambassadors in London, and to British officers of state, which are required by custom after one has handed over one's letters of credit. Everywhere he went, Ribbentrop would assume a well-rehearsed pose and utter the same set speech, very long and full of sound and fury, about the need to fight Communism—which evoked ironical shoulder-shrugging even among those who were sympathetic towards Hitler's Germany. Only when he came to visit me (he was not able to avoid doing so) did Ribbentrop make an exception. For the quarter of an hour which he spent in the Soviet Embassy, the new German Ambassador talked exclusively of the fogs in London.

A few days later I went to pay my return visit to Ribbentrop. And at this point the German side staged the following farcical comedy. On the steps of the German Embassy I was met by a tall, hulking youth with a physiognomy of brazen *hauteur*. He was in civilian clothes, but his bearing, manners and style left no doubt of his Gestapo origins. This youth clicked his heels, stood to attention, and then opened the outer door of the Embassy with a low bow. In the vestibule I was met by a further four youths of the same Gestapo type; they too clicked their heels and stood to attention, and helped me off with my coat. In the reception room where I spent some minutes while Ribbentrop was informed of my arrival, I was entertained by youth No. 6—this one, though, was of a just slightly more intellectual type. On the stairs leading to the second floor, where the Ambassador's study was, stood three more stout Gestapo lads, one at the bottom, one at the top, and one in the middle, and as I walked past them each of them came to attention and loudly clicked his heels. . . .

Which made nine of Himmler's archangels on hand to salute the Soviet Ambassador when he as a matter of diplomatic etiquette paid a visit to the German Ambassador! After that, Ribbentrop spent fifteen minutes ardently assuring me that the British did not know how to rule their amazingly rich Empire. And when we had made our farewells and I proceeded from the German Ambassador's study back to the car I had left waiting outside, the Gestapo parade was repeated once more. The ex-commercial traveller clearly wanted to 'make an impression' on me. One really needed to be quite monstrously stupid, and to have a truly phenomenal lack of understanding of the Soviet psychology, in order to imagine one could 'impress' the Ambassador of the u.s.s.r. by such a farce.

When I got home, I invited some English journalists round and described to them in detail the ritual of my reception at the German Embassy. The journalists guffawed loudly and promised to make this 'sensational news' widely known in political circles in London. They kept their word. For several days all that was talked of round Parliament and in Fleet Street was Maisky being received by Ribbentrop. The incident earned the German Ambassador not laurels but nettles.

Ribbentrop's behaviour in the Committee for 'Non-intervention' was also odd to a degree. When he arrived for a meeting he exchanged greetings with no one, but with a haughtily uninterested expression on his face, as if noticing none of those present, would make his way to his place at the table, and having settled himself in his chair, would direct his piercing gaze up at the ceiling. Even when he had occasion to speak in a meeting he remained in this one unchanging pose, gazing stubbornly at the ceiling. Neither the Chairman nor the other members of the Committee existed for the German Ambassador. It was all so provocatively insolent that even Plymouth did not hide his irritation, and Grandi would glance at his comrade-in-arms with a malicious smile.

The members of the Committee were outraged by Ribbentrop's behaviour, but no one could bring himself to the point of giving him the lesson he deserved. Then I took the initiative myself. At one meeting, when I had to speak immediately after Ribbentrop, I began my speech thus:

'If the German Ambassador would look, instead of seeking inspiration on the ceiling, at the events taking place in real life, then . . .'

—and from there I went on to my real argument.

That was enough. As soon as the words 'inspiration' and 'ceiling' were heard, the German Ambassador came to life, just as if someone had laid a whip across his back. He shifted round in his chair, removed his gaze from the ceiling and began to look round cautiously at those around the table. . . . The ice was broken! From then on Ribbentrop no longer tried to act the part of a stone idol set apart from all surrounding it.

All Ribbentrop's contributions to discussion in the Committee were uncommonly crude, blunt and unskilful. Now and again he would come forward to 'help' Grandi. The Italian Ambassador would just have made a long speech spinning out a cunning web of half-truths and half-lies, of facts re-shuffled or omitted; Plymouth's face would just have assumed that thoughtfully bewildered expression which always denoted that he half agreed with the arguments he had heard; Corbin and Cartier (if the latter was not asleep) would just have started to utter meaningful grunts to indicate that Grandi's ideas really were deserving of serious consideration . . . and bang! Ribbentrop would heave a great rock on to the Committee table, with all the force of his arms! The web Grandi had woven would be torn apart at once, and the whole effect of his carefully worked out concept would be immediately dispelled. Ribbentrop's face would reflect a deep satisfaction—and Grandi's a scarcely concealed fury.

These little ways of Ribbentrop's caused many a laugh among the members of the Committee, and one of the Committee's wits (Masaryk, I suspect) re-named the German Ambassador 'Brickendrop'. The nickname stuck, apt as it was, to the representative of Nazi Germany . . .

Ribbentrop's ignorance and vulgarity often made him look foolish. I remember one incident: during one of my sharp clashes with him I said: 'The great German poet Heinrich Heine says——'

I had not time to finish the phrase before Ribbentrop angrily snarled—not exclaimed, snarled is the exact word—'That is not a German poet!'

Those around the green table at once became alert. I stopped for a moment, and then, looking Ribbentrop straight in the eye, said: 'Ah, really? You disown Heinrich Heine? . . . Very good! The Soviet Union will be very glad to adopt him.'

Loud laughter rang round the table. Ribbentrop reddened and through force of habit turned his eyes up to the ceiling.

To conclude the description of those who played a prominent part in the life of the Committee, I must mention one more figure, that of our general secretary, Francis Hemming. He was a man of 45 or so, unshakably calm, sharply observant. He saw and heard everything that was said at the green-covered table, remembered everything, could produce exhaustive information about everything. As a professional civil servant (for 25 years Hemming had been functioning as a secretary, in many ministries, establishments and organisations) he belonged to no party and did not like expressing his political convictions publicly. In Britain civil servants are by law bound to be non-party, in order that they may work equally well with governments of any composition. In Hemming this principle of non-partisanship went so far that he did not permit himself any definite opinions on any political issue, even in his own mind.

I have already mentioned that Hemming was sympathetic to the Spanish democrats, but this was sympathy in general, without any clear shape. Hemming's brain was so well trained that he could pick up with the greatest of ease the most violently opposed views and find for them exceedingly well 'streamlined' formulations, as a result of which the gulf between them was somehow made invisible, smoothed out.

Hemming was seen in his most special glory when it was time to draw up the official communiqué on the meeting of the Committee or Sub-committee just concluded. A word was enough for him to catch the wishes of each participant in the discussion, which he would instantly clothe in a form of words acceptable to the majority; if there were any objections he would at once make changes, adding something here and taking away something there, and in the end produce a document which satisfied everyone.

Hemming was also an excellent organiser of all the office work (and not only the office work!) of the Committee. If a meeting of the Committee or Sub-committee ended at, say, 6 o'clock in the evening, by 9 o'clock all the participants would receive duplicated copies of the stenographic notes, sent round to their Embassies by messenger. It always struck me as next door to a miracle.

And another example. When the Committee decided to get down to working out the details of the first control plan (which we shall be speaking of in the next chapter), in the space of one week Hemming produced for our consideration not only a draft of such a plan but a whole stack of involved calculations on its financial, administrative and technical execution. In this field Hemming was an absolute wizard, and I more than once paid public tribute to his amazing organisational talents.[1]

1. In particular, at the meeting of the Committee on 9 December 1936, in summing up the results of three months of its work, I declared:
'If and when the future historian ever begins to delve into the work of the Committee, it is hardly likely that he will describe it as a glorious page in the history of post-war diplomacy. For, indeed, if we are to speak frankly and honestly, we must admit that the only really good and splendid work

One more interesting touch. This ideal secretary and administrator had, like many Englishmen, a private hobby totally unconnected with his public duties. Hemming was a passionate amateur entomologist. That same year, 1936, in which he became secretary of the Committee for 'Non-intervention', saw him also elected secretary of an International Commission on Zoological Nomenclature. And in 1938, when the Committee was immersed in working out the second control plan (which will also be spoken of later), Hemming was at the same time acting as general secretary of an International Conference for the protection of African flora and fauna.

Hemming's particular love was South American insects, and a major scientific work which he published about these was highly thought of by professional entomologists.

has been done by . . . the Secretariat of the Committee, which, under the able direction of Mr. Hemming, has been a marvel of organisation and efficiency. As to the Committee itself, however, it must be confessed that it has so far but one achievement to show: a positively amazing talent for performing that drill which is called "marking time".'

8

Words, words——and
mountains of paper

THE idea of checking on the observance of the Agreement on Non-intervention in Spanish affairs was an idea of Soviet origin. The reader already knows that on 12 October 1936, that is, five days after the Soviet government's first protest concerning infringement of the Agreement by the Fascist powers, Lord Plymouth had received our Note demanding the immediate establishment of a watch on Portuguese ports.

Such a demand was in line with the insistent dictates of events. Discussion in the Committee of complaints of violation of the Agreement, without effective checking up, had at once revealed itself as fruitless. And in the end even the representatives of Britain and France were obliged to meet us halfway.

The first practical step was taken by Plymouth on 24 October; the British representative put forward for discussion a proposal to send to Spain 'with the agreement of both parties' a group of neutral persons who could on the Committee's instructions send it the information it needed. And on 2 November it was again Plymouth who placed on the table before the Sub-committee a more fully elaborated control scheme, which had these following points:

1. Two groups of neutral persons to be created, one to be positioned at the main points of entry into Spain (by land and sea) within the territory under the control of the Spanish

Government, while the other should be at similar points on the territory controlled by the rebels.

2. In the interests of observing strict impartiality, the persons composing the two groups should be approved by a plenary meeting of the Committee for 'Non-intervention'.

3. Those belonging to the above-mentioned groups, in both parts of Spain, to have the right to ascertain by all appropriate methods that nothing prohibited by the Agreement on Non-intervention was being imported.

4. Both groups to be instructed to report to the Committee all cases of violation of the Agreement, both on their own initiative and when asked to do so by the Committee.

The governments of the countries represented on the Sub-committee approved the draft in principle, but the details required further elaboration. The meetings of 9, 10 and 12 November were devoted to this, and it was here that Francis Hemming's excellent qualities and those of the secretariat he had created, were seen for the first time in all their glory. As I have already noted, the secretariat contrived to work out with amazing speed and exactitude just where observers would have to be stationed, how many of these would be required altogether, how they could keep in touch with the Committee, what funds would be needed to put the whole control plan into operation, etc., etc.

On 12 November, after a comparatively short debate in the Committee's plenary meeting, the plan was unanimously approved. The total number of personnel required to operate the control plan was set at 1,000, and the rate of expenditure required at approximately £1 million for one year. The Committee's observers on Spanish soil were to have the rights and privileges of diplomatic personnel.

The logic of common sense would have called for the most urgent steps to be taken now to put the approved plan into operation. But this did not happen. Rather peculiar delays began. Only on 23 November did the Sub-committee take the formal decision to send the plan to be considered by 'both parties in Spain', and only on 2 December was this decision ratified by a plenary meeting.[1] In this way 20 days were wasted.

Why?

Light is shed on this by a conversation I had with the Belgian Ambassador Cartier on 12 November—just after the plenary meeting which approved the control plan.

'Well, at last our Committee has done something useful,' I remarked. Cartier waved a contemptuous hand and laughed. 'We shouldn't have wasted so much time and effort on that plan. All to no purpose!'

'Why so?'

'Anyone can see that the war in Spain will be over in a day or two,' explained Cartier with a note of superiority in his voice. 'Another week, and Franco will be master of Spain . . . I assure you, we have been working for nothing. The Observation Scheme will never get beyond the shelves of the diplomatic archives. . . .'

My conversation with Churchill on 5 November came unbidden to mind. Cartier was not at all original in his ideas. . . .

The rebels were still pressing on towards Madrid, fighting was taking place along the Mansanares and in the university town, and the bourgeois world did not believe, did not want to believe, that the Republicans could hold out. They awaited the fall of the Republic from day to day. That was why the Committee for 'Non-intervention', having approved a control plan, was in no hurry to put it into operation. Many people wanted to wait and see: maybe that plan will never need to be put into practice . . . ?

Only by the end of November was it perfectly clear that Franco's advance on Madrid had failed, and that the war in Spain was beginning to assume a character quite other than that which would have suited the bourgeois world. The Committee for 'Non-intervention' realised, sadly, that the control plan would after all have to be tried out in practice. And not only tried out, but

1. At the same time the Committee empowered Plymouth to approach the British government with a request to forward the plan to the recipients (the Spanish government, and Franco) through its diplomatic channels.

bothered over and further improved, for on 4 December the Soviet government came forward with a new, extremely important initiative.

We were the first to reach the conviction that Franco obviously had not got the forces needed to give him victory over the Republic, not even when he was copiously supplied with arms from abroad. For him the ever more insistent question was: where to find soldiers? At that period Franco still did not dare to carry out mass mobilisation in the areas he had occupied—the hatred of the workers and peasants for Fascism was too great! The rebel chief had only one way out: to ask for reinforcements from Germany and Italy. And his requests did not fall on deaf ears. From the second half of November onwards, the Spanish ports occupied by the Falangists began to be invaded by thousands of German 'tourists' and Italian 'volunteers'. Hitler sent Franco mostly aircraft, advisers and instructors, while Mussolini despatched to Spain entire military groupings.[1]

Of course the Soviet Union could not remain indifferent to this extension of German and Italian intervention in Spain, and on 4 December, on instructions from Moscow, I sent Plymouth a letter which declared:

'The recent arrival in Cadiz and other points held by the rebels of thousands of German "volunteers" sent to assist the rebels makes it imperative that some action should immediately be taken by the Committee in order to cope with this problem.

'On the instructions of my Government, therefore, I propose:

'1. To extend the obligations of the Non-intervention Agreement to cover the sending of volunteers to Spain.

'2. That the Governments, parties to the Non-intervention Agreement, shall undertake to prevent by every means the despatch and transit of volunteers to Spain.

1. The Minister for Foreign Affairs of Fascist Italy, Ciano, in a speech made after the end of the Spanish war (16 December 1939), openly admitted: 'At the orders of the Duce himself, an expeditionary force was organised with extreme speed, which then rendered effective aid to the troops of Generalissimo Franco.'

G

'3. That the Governments, parties to the Non-intervention Agreement, shall be approached immediately, through their representatives on the Committee, with the object of obtaining their consent to the extension of the obligations of the Non-intervention Agreement as proposed in paragraphs 1 and 2 above.

'4. That the agents of the Non-intervention Committee to be stationed at the principal points of entry by land and by sea in Spain should be entrusted with the additional duty of controlling the observance of the additional undertakings proposed above by all the parties concerned.'

This Soviet initiative caused great excitement in the Committee. All the 'democratic' powers, headed by Britain and France, supported our proposal, and Francis Hemming was instructed to draft out an appropriate programme of measures by the next meeting. Simultaneously the British government sent to the Committee a communication pointing out that '. . . nationals of foreign Powers are arriving in Spain in ever-increasing numbers to take part in the Spanish Civil War on both sides', and calling for an urgent search for means to stop this.

For a correct understanding of the position of Britain (and of the other 'democratic' powers also) it is essential to bear in mind that at the end of 1936 the London politicians were still trying to stress in every way their neutrality and impartiality in Spanish affairs. The war in the Iberian peninsula was only beginning, and no one knew who would be the victor. The big play with Hitler, of which we spoke earlier, had not yet had time to get fully under way. Another factor having a sensible effect was pressure from their own proletariat on the British leaders, pressure born of sympathy towards the Spanish Republic. In such a situation it was more advantageous to manœuvre, to appear in the guise of an independent 'third force' whose only interest, of course, was the speediest possible re-establishment of peace in the Iberian peninsula. On 23 November 1936, for instance, the British Foreign Secretary Eden, speaking in Parliament, declared:

'The policy of His Majesty's Government is to take no part in the Spanish war and to give no assistance to either side in the struggle.'[1]

Three weeks later, on 18 December, Eden added to this in another speech on the Spanish question the following:

'I should like to see the Government in Spain that Spain wants, and that is the whole motive behind our support of the policy of non-intervention. We think it is the duty of all nations to keep out of this Spanish quarrel and to allow the Spanish people to settle their sufficiently tragic difficulties in their own way.'[2]

At about the same time the British and French governments proposed to the U.S.S.R., Germany and Italy that they should act jointly as mediators between the warring parties in Spain. The Soviet government accepted this proposal, and Hitler and Mussolini rejected it. The result was that the Anglo-French initiative came to nothing. But the very possibility of its taking place was very characteristic of the mood then prevailing in governmental circles in the 'democratic' countries. It was these attitudes which gave rise to the support given by the 'democratic' powers to the Soviet proposal concerning 'volunteers'.

The reaction from the Fascist governments was quite different. The last thing they wanted was the extension of the Agreement on Non-intervention to cover 'volunteers'. But at the same time it was difficult for them to come out openly against the Soviet proposal. So the German and Italian representatives had recourse to a more involved manœuvre: they tried to lose the clear and concrete demand advanced by the U.S.S.R. in a vague fog of words about what they called 'indirect intervention'.

Grandi and Ribbentrop suddenly discovered that the question of 'volunteers' was too narrowly framed, and brought out dozens of new questions.

'What are we to say,' they asked, 'for example, about the

1. Parliamentary Debates, Commons, vol. 319, 23 November 1936. (*Hansard*)
2. Ibid., 18 December 1936.

financial aid which the Republicans are receiving from their sympathisers abroad? What are we to say about the propaganda which the Communists are carrying on in favour of the Spanish Republic all over Europe? What are we to say about various expressions of sympathy with the Spanish Republic which are from time to time to be heard from writers, academics and public figures in other countries?'

And their summing up of the situation was that all the foregoing were different forms of 'indirect intervention', and so to be prohibited.

Particular industry and even art, in its way, was exhibited by Grandi in staging this shadow-play. Ribbentrop merely made noises of assent.

The arguments of the Fascist representatives had their effect, as usual, on Plymouth and Corbin. The result was the passing at the plenary meeting of 9 December 1936 of a resolution of a compromise nature. It recognised in principle the need to extend the Agreement on 'Non-intervention' to cover 'indirect intervention', but noted that the first and most important task in this respect was to combat 'the entry into Spain of foreign nationals for the purpose of taking service in the civil war'.

The Fascist powers thus did not succeed in pushing into the background the question of 'volunteers'. But this could not satisfy the u.s.s.r. Past experience had made me very sceptical about the speed and efficiency of the Committee's workings. For this reason I seized the opportunity to speak, at this same meeting on 9 December, and speak very critically, of the Committee's policy. Exactly three months had passed since its formation, which provided me with an occasion to sum up results.

'. . . the balance-sheet of the Committee's activities during the three months of its existence . . . may be summed up in Hamlet's famous utterance: "Words, words, words!" Yes, words; and in addition to these words, a vast ever-rising mountain of papers, very carefully prepared and delivered to us by the Secretariat. But as to work, real work, what of that? There has simply been no real work done so far.'

After going on to quote a long list of facts in support of this thesis, and stressing the exceptional importance of the 'volunteers' problem, I ended my speech thus:

'I venture to express my hope that at any rate on the question of volunteers the Committee will succeed in achieving some practical results.'

This hope was justified only in part. Thanks to determined sabotage by the Fascist powers and to a suspicious tolerance on the part of Britain and France, the Committee's consideration of the 'volunteers' problem dragged on a weary while, and it was only two months later that a decision was at last taken on the prohibition of 'voluntary service' as from 20 February 1937.

That was how it was formulated on paper. As for how matters stood in fact, we shall see shortly. . . .

Annoyed by their failure over the 'volunteers', the Fascist powers tried to get their own back in other ways. On 12 January 1937 Ribbentrop and Grandi raised at a meeting of the Sub-committee the question of the 'Spanish gold'. The Fascist representatives began to demand that by way of combating 'indirect intervention' the Committee should establish control over the disposition of the gold reserves held by the Republic in foreign banks. The sense of the proposal was clear: to help 'Non-intervention' to get its paws on at least that part of the Spanish gold fund which was kept in London and Paris, and so make it even more difficult for the Republic to acquire abroad the arms it so badly needed.

The Soviet government came out firmly against this project. For a long time Ribbentrop and Grandi refused to give up. At the Sub-committee's meetings of 18 January, 2 and 22 February, 1, 8, 16 and 23 March, 28 April, and 18 May they returned again and again to the 'Spanish gold'. Under their pressure Plymouth and Corbin, who at first had reacted negatively to the Fascist proposal (after all, this touched the sacred rights of property!), began to 'weaken' somewhat, and even got through the Sub-committee a decision to set up a 'special commission of lawyers' which was to work out 'a compromise acceptable to all'.

It became clear that the representatives of the 'democratic' powers were prepared to go a long way in making concessions to Ribbentrop and Grandi; serious danger threatened the resources abroad of the Spanish government. But the u.s.s.r. remained unshakable, and since all the Committee's decisions had to be taken unanimously, nothing came of the Fascist powers' evil intent. Ribbentrop and Grandi did not even risk putting the matter to a vote. The 'Spanish gold' remained in the hands of the Spanish government . . .

But I am running on too fast once again. I return now to the description of events in their chronological order.

On 2 December, then, the Committee addressed to the British government its request that the latter bring to the knowledge of 'both the parties in Spain' the control plan for checking observance of the Agreement on Non-intervention. It was twenty days before even preliminary replies were received from the Spanish government and from General Franco. On 23 December 1936 these documents were considered by the Committee at a plenary meeting.

The reply from the Spanish government, full of dignity, was of a conciliatory nature. Stressing the democratic legality of its powers and the fact of its international recognition, the Republican government energetically defended its right to buy abroad the arms it needed to suppress rebellion. At the same time it declared that the government was prepared to meet the Committee half-way and afford it 'every facility for discovering the violators of the Agreement'.

Franco's reply, prompted of course by the Fascist powers, had quite another ring. To give the reader a clearer impression of this subject, I will allow myself to quote some passages from my own speech at the plenary meeting of 23 December:

'. . . To the vast accumulation of the Committee's documents he has added one which I can only describe as a compound of folly and insolence.

'Instead of giving a definite reply as to whether or not he accepts the proposed scheme—even in principle—this pocket

general is graciously pleased to tell us that he "will continue to
study the Non-intervention Committee's communication".'

I proceeded to point out that the newly revealed 'Fuehrer' had
had no hesitation in 'reprimanding' the British government,
which had acted merely as postman between him and the Committee, and then I went on to the questions which Franco had
addressed to the Committee itself:

'. . . For instance, he asks: "Are the Non-intervention
Committee's agents to concern themselves only with the entry
of war material into Spain, or are they also to withdraw from the
fronts the large stocks of arms bought with the gold stolen from
the Bank of Spain, and with the proceeds of other robberies
from banks and private houses? . . . Does the Non-intervention
Committee intend to establish agents in French port towns
which are now centres of supply and recruitment for the various
Red pseudo-governments and which nourish the anarchy that
reigns in the territory not yet occupied by the National Army?"
—And so on. What language! What expressions! . . .'

It was perfectly apparent from Franco's reply that the rebels
did not agree to admit the Committee's observers to the territory
they held. *Ipso facto* there collapsed the whole organisational
basis on which the control plan rested.

One might have thought that the natural consequence of this
would be a decision to take emergency action to alter the plan, in
view of the impossibility of applying it in its first form. But the
Committee did not do so. Corbin made a proposal, that those
powers who had influence 'in one or other of the Spanish camps'
should use it to try and get the control plan accepted as it stood.
The French Ambassador was supported by all the other members
of the Committee (except me), after which followed the decision
to give 'both parties in Spain' time to think about it, and to
await their final replies.

These final replies, which as might have been expected contained nothing new as against the preliminary ones, arrived on
the Committee table, or rather the Sub-committee table, only on
28 January 1937. Having thus lost over a month in fruitless

delay, the Sub-committee saw fit at last to begin working out a new control scheme.

But here the question arose, what was to be re-cast, and how, from the old scheme, now useless thanks to Franco's opposition? The discussion revolved around this in the Sub-committee meeting of 28 January and in the end unanimous agreement was reached that control points should be established along the land and sea borders of Spain, but outside of Spanish territory itself. In concrete terms this meant that on land the Committee's control posts would have to be set up on the territory of France and Portugal, and at sea patrols of warships, from the fleets of countries participating in the work of the Committee, would have to cruise constantly at a certain agreed distance outside Spanish territorial waters.

The indefatigable Francis Hemming, who had noted a number of symptoms foretelling the impossibility of the control plan ever being applied in its original form, had prepared in advance a second version, on the general lines of the conclusions reached by the Committee on 28 January. After consideration of this new version, the Sub-committee adjudged it satisfactory, and instructed the secretariat to prepare with the greatest possible speed a detailed elaboration of the scheme as outlined, though the representatives of the Fascist powers again tried to create as many difficulties and obstacles as possible.

I shall here mention only the two most extreme cases.

The first of these concerned Portugal. Inspired by Rome and Berlin, she categorically refused to admit the Committee's observing officers to her territory. For three weeks unsuccessful negotiations went on between the Committee and the Portuguese government. Most probably they would have ended in nothing, if a hand in the matter had not been taken by Britain—the traditional patron of Portugal. The result was that a compromise was reached: the Portuguese government agreed to admit about 130 control officers, but only in the capacity of agents of the British government (not of the Committee) and only if they were all of British nationality.

These agents were to be subordinate to the British Ambassador in Lisbon, and to maintain contact with the Committee only through him.

The second case concerns the U.S.S.R. As has been mentioned above, the new version of the plan provided for naval patrols around Spain. But which powers were to take part in the patrolling? Ribbentrop and Grandi insisted that only Britain, France, Germany and Italy were to be allowed to share in this. The Fascists objected strongly to warships of the U.S.S.R. being included in patrol duties. The Soviet government, on the contrary, demanded on principle its full equality of rights in this respect. Plymouth and Corbin took up a very dubious position; while not lining up openly with the Fascist representatives, they at the same time avoided directly supporting the U.S.S.R. Debates on this point in the Committee and Sub-committee took up almost the whole of February. However, the firmness displayed by the Soviet government obliged all its enemies, open and concealed, to retreat. In the last resort the Committee took a decision that participation in naval patrol work was open to all powers who had signed the Agreement on Non-intervention. The U.S.S.R. had thus gained a victory of principle. But then something happened which the Committee was not expecting. At a meeting of the Sub-committee on 26 February, I made on behalf of the Soviet government the following statement:

'. . . in view of the fact that it has now been agreed in principle that any Government which is a party to the Non-intervention Agreement has the right, should they so desire, to participate in the naval supervision scheme, the U.S.S.R. Government does not claim at present to make actual use of this right, as it is not interested either politically or otherwise in the presence of its naval forces in the Mediterranean Sea or in the Atlantic Ocean, at a great distance from their own naval bases'.

When I read out this declaration a bewildered and suspicious silence reigned for the first moment around the table of the Sub-committee. Then a sigh of relief broke involuntarily from many chests, and my Swedish neighbour, Palmstierna, shook my hand under the table and whispered: 'Your government has manœuvred really brilliantly. . . .'

The real reason for our refusal of actual participation in naval patrolling was that we had no bases of our own near Spain, and did not wish to make use of French or British bases because as things then stood we feared possible provocatory incidents, which would have made the international atmosphere even more heated. In the circumstances then obtaining we were quite satisfied with the recognition in principle of our equal right to take part in patrolling near Spanish territorial waters.

We succeeded in gaining some further victories, also. After prolonged pressure on the part of the u.s.s.r., on 16 February 1937 a plenary meeting of the Committee took two very important decisions: to prohibit the passage to Spain of any 'volunteers' whatsoever as from 21 February 1937; and to bring the observation scheme into operation by sea and on land on the night of 6–7 March.

From this moment the Sub-committee plunged into feverish activity. Suffice it to say that between 16 February and 8 March there were 12 meetings of the Sub-committee, over and above which there were various commissions and sub-commissions working non-stop. Not for nothing did Plymouth declare on Monday 8 March, when reporting to the full Committee on the final version of the fully elaborated control plan, and speaking with a mixture of regret and pride: 'We worked till a late hour on Saturday evening . . .' He could find no better proof of the uncommon industry of the Sub-committee. How could he, indeed? The sacred English weekend had been jettisoned, the games of golf and cricket (with which British politicians and statesmen commonly recreate themselves at this time) had been forgotten. What more could one say!

The plenary meeting of 8 March, which met both morning and afternoon, itself provided an interesting picture in the light of subsequent events. Of course the control plan was accepted unanimously and practically without discussion. Of course the representatives of Britain and France made very optimistic speeches in this connection. This was so to speak in the nature of things. Less usual was the behaviour of the German and Italian representatives. No one could fail to note that for so important a meeting of the Committee both Ribbentrop and Grandi had failed to put in an appearance. They were deputised for by persons of secondary rank—Counsellor of the Embassy Woermann for Germany, and Counsellor of the Embassy Crolla for Italy. This gave food for some thought. On the other hand, as if to ward off any possible doubts, the two Counsellors both went into the most immoderate ecstasies when they spoke. They even tried to bring in sweeping attributions of credit to the Fascist powers for initiative and rights of authorship in the production of the control plan.

Counsellor Woermann among other remarks said:

'My government sincerely hope that the measures which are about to be put into operation will contribute towards making an end as soon as possible to the unhappy and cruel civil war which brings such great sufferings to the Spanish people and to other countries too . . . I am especially glad that the question of volunteers, first raised in August 1936 by the German, Italian and Portuguese Governments, has now found a solution. Unfortunately, it has not yet been possible to fix the exact date on which the control plan as a whole will be put definitely into force, and I hope we will arrange as soon as possible to find a definite date for the beginning of control . . . The German Government have expressed from the very beginning the desire that every Power should abstain from intervening in the present conflict in Spain.'

The Italian counsellor, Crolla, also spoke in the same vein.

Unlike all the other members of the Committee, I spoke very cautiously at the meeting of 8 March. My speech contained a good deal of scepticism, which flowed naturally enough from experience of the past work of the Committee. I too expressed satisfaction that the control plan had at last been accepted, but I stressed that the most important thing was to make it a reality by *practical action*, on the matter of 'volunteers' first of all.

'. . . you must all have noticed,' I said, 'that the tendency in our work is to proceed ever more slowly with every new question. It took us about a month to elaborate the first scheme of control which was eventually abandoned because of opposition from General Franco; and it took nearly double that time to elaborate our present scheme for control outside Spain. It is much to be hoped that this progressive doubling will not accompany our arrangement of a scheme for evacuating the foreign nationals now in Spain . . .'

And here I felt it my duty to give the following warning:

'. . . the Soviet Government now, as previously, can only feel itself bound by the decisions of this Committee provided that such decisions are fully honoured by all the States Members of the Committee. In any other circumstances it will consider itself morally free to reserve freedom of action in this matter.'

At the moment of pronouncing those words I did not myself suspect just how timely and necessary they were.

What exactly was the new control plan now ratified by the Committee?

Its main features were as follows: The whole system of control by land and sea was to be operated under the direct guidance of a special board, consisting of the representatives of Britain, France, the u.s.s.r., Germany, Italy, and three lesser powers (Poland, Greece and Norway). This council was empowered to decide all questions of an administrative or organisational nature. Questions of principle and policy were to be passed back to the Committee for 'Non-Intervention'.

The Franco-Spanish frontier (or the French side of it) was divided into a number of zones; each zone was under observation by a special 'administrator', while the frontier as a whole was under the surveillance of a 'chief administrator'. The control agents working under the 'administrator' were to be stationed at the main points on the roads and railways leading from France into Spain. Over and above these, it was proposed that 'mobile groups' of control officers should be created.

One 'administrator' and a small group of officers were to operate in Gibraltar.

Control on the Spanish-Portuguese border was to be operated on the basis of a special agreement between Britain and Portugal, the general sense of which is already known to the reader.

All the control agents were to have normal diplomatic privileges, also the right of free access and inspection at railway stations, warehouses, elevators, etc. They could demand from the local authorities the documents needed to establish the nature of freight entering Spain, and could check the passports of people travelling in that direction.

All vessels (except naval vessels) sailing under the flags of nations adhering to the Agreement on Non-intervention and bound for Spanish ports (including those in the Spanish zone of Morocco), were to call *en route* at one of eleven named ports (Dover, Cherbourg, Lisbon, Gibraltar, Marseilles, Palermo, etc.) and there pick up two or more of the Committee's observing officers. It was the duty of these officers to observe, without leaving the vessel, the unloading of the ship in the Spanish port. These officers had the right to demand the documents relating to the cargo from the captain of the ship in which they sailed, to question the passengers and crew, and, again, to check passports.

Naval patrolling along the Spanish coast was to be introduced, by warships from Britain, France, Germany and Italy. The whole coast, including that of Spanish Morocco and the Balearic Isles, was divided into seven zones. The British and French vessels were to patrol the Franco-held coast, and the German and Italian vessels the zones held by the Republicans. Patrolling was to be at a distance of 10 miles from the coast. The patrol vessels did not have the right to search cargo ships bound for Spain. Their task was merely to ascertain whether observing officers of the Committee were on board.

The total number of personnel manning the control system (observing officers, administrators, staff of the central council, etc.) was, as before, 1,000 persons. They were all to be recruited in given proportions from citizens of the 13 countries adhering to the Agreement on Non-intervention. In charge of the central council, and with his headquarters in London, was a Dutch Rear-

Admiral (retired), Van Dulm; chief administrator for naval control was another Dutch Rear-Admiral (retired), Olivier, and chief administrator for land control in France was a Dane, Colonel Lunn. The post of Secretary of the central board and Accounting Officer of the international monetary fund was given to Francis Hemming.

The sum allocated to running the control system, for a period of one year, was £898,000, 80 per cent of which was to be provided by Britain, France, the u.s.s.r., Germany and Italy (£144,000 each), while the remaining 20 per cent was divided among the other, smaller countries adhering to the Agreement.

It is hardly necessary to point out that the control plan outlined above had many shortcomings. It did not extend to the Canary Islands, for instance, or to the Spanish colonies in Africa, through which the traffic in arms and war materials could pass to continental Spain. It did not extend to men-of-war, or to vessels sailing under non-European flags or under the Spanish flag (whether Republican or Francoite). It also left aside transport by air.

None the less, the control plan accepted on 8 March 1937 could have served a certain purpose, if it had been quickly brought into action and efficiently operated. Italian and German intervention would have come up against considerable difficulties, in that case. But for that very reason the control plan was immediately dogged by 'bad luck'.

9

Exposure of a Fascist myth

THE three months separating the collapse of the Fascist advance on Madrid and the ratification by the Committee of the control plan had been a period of relative quiet on the front and of great activity in consolidation of forces in the rear, on both sides.

The Fascists were going through a serious reappraisal of values. No one doubted any more that Franco and his own forces (that is the Spanish rebels, plus the 'foreign legion' and the Moroccans) were incapable of conquering the Republic, even when being plentifully supplied with arms from abroad. Hitler and Mussolini were faced with a dilemma: should they let Fascism be defeated in Spain, or support Franco not only with arms but by sending him major military formations. The question was decided in favour of raising their stakes in intervention. By February 1937 the total number of Italians fighting for Franco reached about 60,000, and the number of Germans about 10,000.

Military aid to the rebels was supplemented by political and diplomatic support. On 21 November 1936 Germany and Italy recognised Franco's 'government', having first broken off diplomatic relations with the Spanish Republic. A week later, that is on 28 November, Italy concluded a secret agreement with Franco which provided for close co-operation of the two parties to the Agreement in international policy, in the utilisation of Spain's natural resources, and even in 'the restoration of social and political order' in Spanish territory. At the beginning of 1937 the Fascist camp was more full of aggressive spirit than ever.

But consolidation was going on in the camp of democracy too. The revolutionary people is a mighty force. Its works are always abundant, ingenious, richly varied. So it was in Spain also. Once the people had risen to the defence of the Republic it performed real miracles of endurance and unexampled heroism, in spite of the most enormous obstacles and difficulties. In the van, as always in such cases, marched the Communist Party.

On 18 December 1936 a declaration by the Party appeared in the newspaper *Mundo Obrero* under the heading 'The Eight Conditions for Victory'. These eight conditions were as follows:

That the full measure of power be assured to the government, which represented all the social forces of the country and reflected the will of the masses;

that universal obligatory military service be introduced, a unified command and general staff be created, and officers loyal to the Republic and the people brought forward to lead the armed forces;

that iron discipline be established in the rear of the troops;

that the main branches of industry be nationalised and re-organised, the armaments industry first of all;

that workers' control over production be organised;

that fair prices be fixed for agricultural products, and production plans for industry and agriculture co-ordinated.

It is somewhat superfluous to say that numerous obstacles barred the way to the practical realisation of this programme, obstacles which were not fully overcome right up to the end of the war. But the logic of events and the energy of the Communist Party helped to ensure that the Spanish Republic did move forward along this road, step by step, even if in wavering and zigzag fashion.

During the three-month lull at the front, the best progress of all was made in the reorganisation of the armed forces. The famous Fifth Regiment became the skeleton on which was built up the new Republican army. By governmental order, the transformation of the militia into regular troops was to be completed by 7 January 1937. In actual fact this happened somewhat later.

But it was at the meeting-point of the two years 1936 and 1937, that decisive successes were scored in the creation of a real, revolutionary-democratic army for Spain.

The birth of the new army was attended by all manner of difficulties. It was continually slowed down by Largo Caballero on the one hand and the Anarcho-syndicalists on the other.

Largo Caballero, who held the joint offices of Premier and Minister of Defence, had, as we have seen, fallen under the influence of the old military experts. Among these last, mediocrities predominated, and there were some direct agents of Franco. The net result was that Largo Caballero began to pipe to their tune. He opposed the creation of a general staff and a unified command, took a negative attitude to the institution of military commissars,[1] and repeated all the time that the army should have as little as possible to do with politics.

The Anarcho-syndicalists for their part also refused to be reconciled to the need for centralisation, and put up a long fight against the strict discipline which is essential for any battle-worthy army. They were shouting aloud at every street corner that the creation of such an army was a betrayal of the cause of revolution. The Anarcho-syndicalists on principle objected to going beyond the people's militia that had come into being in the first days of the war.

In September 1936, when the Catalan government called two age-groups to the colours, the National Confederation of Labour —the main stronghold of the Anarcho-syndicalists—promptly called a huge meeting in Barcelona, at which the following slogan was proclaimed: 'People's Militia—Yes! Soldiers of the regular army—No!' With this slogan on their lips the Anarcho-syndicalists attacked the barracks where the new recruits were, and made them go back to their homes.

The consequence of this state of affairs was that the creation of a regular Republican army proceeded relatively slowly and very

1. The institution of military commissars was only introduced in the Republican Army on 16 October 1936. Largo Caballero signed the decree on this under pressure from the popular masses.

H

unevenly. As a rule, the process advanced better and more quickly in those places which were nearer to the front, and those where the influence of the Communist Party was greater. In the neighbourhood of Madrid and in the south, near Posoblanco, by February–March 1937 there was already a comparatively large, disciplined and battle-ready army, but in Catalonia, Levant and, especially, Malaga, where the Anarcho-syndicalists played an unusually important role, the armed forces of the Republic still consisted of an insufficiently organised and badly led mass of People's Militiamen, incapable of putting up serious resistance to the enemy's regular troops.

During this same three-month period the International Brigades also grew considerably larger and stronger. The idea of creating such brigades had arisen quite spontaneously. It began with anti-Fascists resident in Spain, who immediately following 18 July 1936 declared their desire to take part in the fight against Franco. Then from over the Pyrenees came Frenchmen who wanted to do battle with German and Italian Fascism not in words only but arms in hand. They were followed by émigrés who had found a refuge in France from Fascism or semi-Fascism in their own countries—Germans, Italians, Poles. And from the end of August onwards the movement for the creation of International Brigades assumed an all-European and even world-wide character, under the influence of the world's democratic forces springing to the aid of the Spanish Republic. The people who wanted to fight Fascism in Spain were volunteers in the best sense of the word. Most of them came from proletarian or intellectual circles. Often, in leaving for the war they had left their families unprovided for. They had not enough money to get to Spain, and many were obliged to make at least part of the journey on foot.

The French government put every conceivable obstacle in the way of the anti-Fascist volunteers on their way to Spain. They had to make their way along the mountain paths of the Pyrenees in the dark of night. Not all the volunteers by any means were Communists. Among them one could find Socialists and Radicals, and people of no party and former pacifists. No one was barred, so long as he showed himself willing to take up arms and fight Fascism.

Between September 1936 and February 1937 15,000 people of 32 different nationalities joined the International Brigades. This variegated pattern of nationalities among the volunteers created certain difficulties. Those organising the brigades tried, naturally, to make up units out of people speaking the same language. This was how the German Thaelmann battalion came into being, the Italian Garibaldi battalion, the French 'Paris Commune' battalion, the Polish Dombrowski battalion and the American Abraham Lincoln battalion. But it was not always possible to bring volunteers of one nationality together in the same battalion. Sometimes multi-national battalions were created. Such, for instance, was the 49th or Chapayev battalion, which included representatives of over 20 nationalities.

Usually, each International Brigade consisted of three battalions, numbering 1,500–2,000 altogether. Five brigades were organised in all. The total number of International Brigaders varied considerably from time to time over the duration of the war, but never exceeded 20,000 (including reserves and reinforcements). Their base was the town of Albacete.

The International Brigades were transformed with fantastic speed into first-class fighting units—disciplined, excellently organised, full of courage and spirit. It was not just a coincidence that the reactionaries both within Spain and outside it got so busy spreading lying rumours to the effect that the majority of those in the International Brigades were professional soldiers. In actual fact the reverse was the case; only a few of the brigaders had had any military training previously. The overwhelming majority had never had a rifle in their hands before. But their burning hatred of Fascism, their revolutionary enthusiasm and their consciousness of the threat hanging over Europe soon made real soldiers out of these inexperienced (militarily speaking) people.

The International Brigades played a particularly important role in the first period of the war, when the Republican army had not yet outgrown its nappy or People's Militia stage. The best example of this role can be seen in the defence of Madrid. But in all the later progress of the war, when the Republican army had already become an impressive military force, the International Brigades took a glorious part in all the major battles—on the Jarama, at Guadalajara, Posoblanco, Brunete, Teruel and lastly on the Ebro. And though the purely military significance of the International Brigades gradually diminished as the Republican army expanded and grew stronger, the immense political significance of these brigades remained as great as ever right to the end. The presence of these brigades at the front was a daily reminder to the Spanish people that the best and most progressive part of the human race was on its side. At the same time it was a demonstration to the working masses all over the world that forces capable of resisting Fascism had already taken shape and were growing rapidly stronger, within the ranks of the proletarian movement.

During these same 3 months the Republic also succeeded in replenishing its arsenals, to some extent at least. Arms came from three main sources. First, an immense expenditure of effort succeeded in getting under way home production of rifles, machine-guns and other light arms.[1] Secondly, since at the beginning of the war the mechanism of 'Non-intervention' was still only in process of creation, there were still some channels left open through which the Republic could obtain—at prohibitive prices, it was true—arms and ammunition from the capitalist countries. And, thirdly and lastly, a comparatively small stream of arms—including tanks and aeroplanes—came from the Soviet Union. From October 1936 to September 1937 only 23 shipments of arms went by sea from the U.S.S.R. to the Spanish Republic.

1. This source would undoubtedly have yielded more perceptible results if the Anarcho-syndicalists had not enjoyed such influence in industrial Catalonia. Owing to them, a considerable part of the war production turned out there 'settled down' locally and found its way into the 'private' arsenals of the Anarchist groups, instead of to the decisive sectors of the front

But all this was very little! Too little, compared to the needs of the Republican army. Too little, compared to what Franco was getting from Germany and Italy.

The Soviet government could, of course, have chosen to make a considerable increase in its deliveries of arms to Spain. The Republic had sufficient means at its disposal to have paid for such deliveries. The limiting factor was the difficulty of transporting them.[1]

By one means or the other, though, by March 1937 the Republican army was considerably better armed than it had been in the first battles before Madrid.

During the 3 months of which we are speaking some events of importance took place in the internal life of the Spanish Republic. The greatest of these was the agrarian reform, carried through by the Communist Minister of Agriculture, Uribe. The Decree on this reform had been proclaimed as early as October 1936, but it was only at the start of the following year that it began to be carried into practice and to become part of the life of the countryside, through the agrarian committees which were set up there.

According to the Decree, the lands of gentry and other landowners 'who directly or indirectly had taken part in the rebellion against the Republic' were liable to confiscation. In practice this meant almost all the landowners' estates came within the scope of the Degree. And in fact about 5 million hectares of land were redistributed among agricultural labourers and small peasants, over the whole war period.

Article 4 of the Decree laid down that the question of how the confiscated land was to be exploited—collectively or individually —was to be decided by specially summoned meetings of the peasantry. Actually the greater part of the expropriated land remained under private ownership. But in some places (notably in Andalusia) collective cultivation also took place; about 1,000

---

1. Interesting details on the transport of arms from the u.s.s.r. to Spain may be found in a paper by N. Nikolayev, 'The Spanish Fleet in the National Revolutionary War of 1936–9,' published in a collecta *From the History of the Liberation Struggle of the Spanish People* (u.s.s.r. Academy of Sciences 1959).

agricultural co-operatives made their appearance in the Republic.

It can easily be understood what an immense effect this reform had on the morale and fighting spirit of the Republican army, which was made up for the most part of peasants. The disappearance of the landowners from the scheme of things and the redivision of their lands was the age-old dream of the Spanish peasantry come true.

Considerable changes took place in industry also. When the war began, all the major industrialists and the majority of the lesser ones abandoned their establishments in Republican territory and fled, either to join Franco or out of the country. The engineering and technical personnel divided into two groups: some followed their masters, others stayed where they were. So life itself dictated the need for important reforms here. The 'orphaned' private factories passed into the hands of the state, the municipalities or, most often, the trade unions. This was not a formal nationalisation of industry, to which the Anarcho-syndicalists expressed the most violent objection. It was just an *incautación* or requisitioning (a term widely employed in Spain at that time). That is, the mills and factories passed into the control of the state or of the public bodies without any final decision being taken as to whose property they would be in the future. Such *incautación* assumed sweeping proportions from the very first months of the war, taking in tens of thousands of enterprises. Difficulties arose in plenty—financial, administrative and organisational. Industry functioned only sporadically (for which the Anarcho-syndicalists must bear the main responsibility). Supplies of industrial goods to the front and in the rear flowed extremely haltingly. None the less, the Spanish worker felt himself the master of the production process for the very first time, and this also worked in no small degree to strengthen the army's morale.

Lastly, the wide international support for republican Spain, the ardent sympathy reaching out to her from democrats at all the ends of the earth, played a huge part in raising up the spirit of the Spanish Republic. Mass meetings protesting against Fascist intervention took place in London, Paris, Stockholm, Mexico

City, and other capitals. The most outstanding scientists and scholars, writers, and other representatives of artistic and cultural life, published anti-Fascist appeals. In all five continents funds were collected to help the working people of Spain. Ships loaded with food and consumer goods set sail for Spain from the U.S.S.R., Britain and France. . . .

All this and much else beside was a visible demonstration that the Spanish people were not alone in their heroic struggle, that they had many friends in other countries, that the world saw them as the vanguard of democracy, ready to repel the black forces of Fascism.

The energetic assistance rendered by the U.S.S.R. was especially important to Spain. I have already related how the Soviet government began to supply the Republican army with arms from October 1936. In the Soviet Union there were people to be found, too, who desired to take part in the struggle against Fascism proceeding on the territory of Spain. Soviet volunteers became part of the Republican army and did it inestimable service.

A very prominent part was played by Soviet journalists and writers also. In particular, the names of Mikhail Koltsov and Ilya Ehrenburg are inseparably bound up with the struggle of the Spanish people. Their despatches from Madrid, and from the Aragonese and other fronts, were reprinted then by the press of the entire world. Koltsov's *Spanish Diary* still remains today an inimitably vivid depiction of events great and small in the Spanish war, and of the heroic defenders of the Republic, their feelings and their attitudes. . . .

By the time that the Committee for 'Non-intervention' ratified the control plan, then, the Spanish Republic was considerably stronger and more solidly grounded than it had been 3 months before. But neither Franco, nor Hitler, nor Mussolini believed this. They had not noticed, or rather did not want to notice, the changes taking place on the far side of the front.

A factor which contributed more than a little to the mistaken impression of the Fascist leaders was the following circumstance.

In mid-January 1937 a column of stranglers of the Republic—20,000 Italian 'volunteers' and 10,000 Spaniards and Moroccans —began to advance upon Malaga. Through the fault of Largo Caballero the Republic still had no regular army there, and the defence of Malaga in fact devolved upon the Anarcho-syndicalist militia (the Anarchists had always been strong in that area). To this was added treason on the part of some military experts who had been commissioned to take charge of military operations in Malaga. The defence of Malaga was organised as badly as it could have been; the mountain gorges around the town were left uncovered, arms were not brought up in time, the troops were not prepared for battle. It is scarcely surprising that the advance of the Fascists from the direction of Algeciras was exceptionally rapid, and Malaga fell on 8 February.

The loss of Malaga, where the Fascists, after the battle was already over, made a bloody slaughter in which over 10,000 peaceful citizens were annihilated, was felt most painfully throughout the country. The prestige of the Anarcho-syndicalists suffered a heavy blow. In Valencia, where the Republican government had its seat at that time, there was a gigantic demonstration demanding the creation of a disciplined, battle-worthy army.

The ease with which the Fascists finally took Malaga confirmed them in their belief that they had quite enough forces at their disposal to smash the Republic completely, and in the very immediate future at that. Again, as on the eve of the first advance on Madrid, Franco felt himself the victor already, and in the Committee for 'Non-intervention' Grandi was again giving everyone to understand that the day was not far distant when the rebel general would ride into the capital as a conqueror on a white horse.

But something happened which they did not expect.

Remembering only too well what a miserable failure the frontal attack on Madrid in November 1936 had been, Franco attempted to gain his object by other means. At the end of January 1937 the rebels began to attack to the south of Madrid, on the river Jarama (a tributary of the Manzanares), intending to outflank the capital. But this new plan too soon began to split at the seams, for, as has been mentioned above, the Republicans here had succeeded in bringing into being a battle-worthy army comparatively quickly. The resistance the rebels met on the Jarama was much more effective than that before Malaga. More than that: by the middle of February it appeared that the initiative was passing into the hands of the Republicans, who mounted a counter-offensive. And by the end of that month the Fascists had to retire to their original positions.

And if Franco failed to achieve his objective on the Jarama, the subsequent attack mounted by the Fascists and the interventionists from the north, across Guadalajara province, proved a positive catastrophe for them, all the more unexpected since there they had seemed to have every chance of winning a decisive victory. During February the enemies of the Republic had got together in the Seguenza area a powerful striking force: four Italian divisions and one Spanish division—about 60,000 men altogether. The Italian corps had 250 guns, 140 tanks and 60 aeroplanes. The general plan of the operation provided for an average rate of advance of 25 kilometres per 24 hours. The start of the attack was to be on 8 March, and the victory parade in Madrid on the 15th.

But fate had a cruel laugh at the expense of the interventionists. On the first day of the attack they advanced, instead of 25 kilometres, only about 5–7, and that with great difficulty. Worse was to follow. The Republican command, making a timely assessment of the fresh threat hanging over the capital, quickly concentrated in the direction of Guadalajara something in the region of 30,000 troops, with 40 guns, 54 tanks and 70 aeroplanes. Of course, even after that was done the forces on either side were far from evenly balanced. But by 12 March, no later, the rebel advance was halted. A great part in this was played by the brilliant flying of the Republican air force: taking off into rain and snow, they successfully bombed the Italian divisions stranded in the mountain passes.

On 13 March the Republicans went over to the attack here also. Giving way before their pressure, the Italians began to retreat, a retreat which very quickly (again thanks to the successful action of the Republican air forces) turned into a general rout.

On 18–19 March the Republicans brought their tank reserves into battle, and came down upon the Italian corps with such force that within 48 hours the latter was completely smashed. Mussolini's 'legionaries', which he had advertised the world over as fearless heroes, were now like hunted hares. They ran for it, abandoning their arms and ammunition as they went.

The Fascist losses in dead and captured were over 10,000 men. The Republican losses were only half as many. Into the hands of Madrid's defenders fell quantities of enemy artillery, machine-guns, rifles, tanks, lorries and all manner of military supplies. Among the staff documents captured was a most interesting telegram from Mussolini, sent from Rome just before the battle began. In it the Italian dictator sent his best wishes for success to his 'gallant heroes' and expressed his complete confidence in their triumph. . . .

The victory of the Republicans at Guadalajara finally cured Franco of any desire to storm Madrid. Right up to the end of the war the Fascists made no further attempt to renew operations of any significance here.

This victory is also usually considered as the baptism by fire of the new, just created, Republican army, which here demonstrated its fighting qualities for all to see.

The victory of Guadalajara was of very great international significance too. The prestige of the Spanish Republic rose at once. Mussolini's prestige, on the other hand, suffered a grave blow. For many years the Italian dictator had been blackmailing Europe with his brazen gesticulation and shouting about the 'military invincibility' of Fascism. And suddenly his divisions at Guadalajara, on coming up for the first time against the army of another European state—even though it was an army only just created, still inexperienced, and badly armed—had been put to shameful flight!

The Fascist myth was then and there exposed.

10

Crisis of the Committee
for 'Non-Intervention'

The Committee's ratification of the control plan, then, coincided with the beginning of the battle of Guadalajara. Ribbentrop and Grandi were at that point concerned about one thing only: to prevent the flow of arms from the U.S.S.R. to the Republicans, and the reinforcement of the international brigades, from altering the balance of forces in Franco's disfavour. That was why the German and Italian representatives had voted so readily for the control plan at the 8 March meeting.

Then all of a sudden the Fascists suffer a catastrophic setback at Guadalajara. It became apparent that the forces and supplies previously brought over to support Franco were not sufficient. The rebels needed new, large-scale supplies of men and arms. But in the meantime a control plan had been accepted, which with all its defects would have hindered the further development of German and Italian intervention considerably. And the plan had been accepted with the active support of Germany and Italy!

The Fascist powers were thus faced with an exceptionally ticklish situation. What were they to do? Come out openly against the control plan, ten days after they had been all in favour of it? No, this would have meant the final exposure of the true face of the Fascist powers, and could have turned even Britain and France against them, let alone the smaller European countries. An open *volte-face* against the plan was impossible in March 1937.

Hitler and Mussolini took a different way out; they began a prolonged and stubborn campaign of sabotage of the *introduction in
practice* of the control plan. The forms of sabotage changed, but
its essence remained constant.

It began at the meeting of the Sub-committee on 16 March,
when the Fascist defeat at Guadalajara had already taken un-
mistakable shape; Grandi suddenly declared that he could not
take part in the elaboration of a detailed plan for the evacuation
of foreign combatants[1] from Spain before a settlement was
reached on the question of the 'Spanish gold'. Counsellor of the
German Embassy Woermann, who was deputising for Ribbentrop at this meeting, immediately lined up with him.

A week later, on 23 March, an even more typical scene was
enacted in the Sub-committee. Grandi, who had evidently
received exhaustive details of the rout of the Italians at Guadalajara, arrived for the meeting in a state of extreme irritability.
Looking at him I could not refrain from thinking 'Aha, now may
we not be able to get some good out of this?'

It was absolutely clear to me that as a result of the disaster at
Guadalajara the Fascist powers' attitude to the control plan had
changed sharply, but for the time being they were still trying to
keep themselves covered by an outer husk of well-worn phrases
about 'non-intervention' and 'resisting intervention'. There had
been no direct declaration to the effect that Germany and Italy
did not want to get out of Spain. And this, of course, made it
more difficult to develop an effective campaign against the
Fascist 'volunteers'. I decided that, in view of the mood Grandi
was in, it was worth trying to get a direct admission out of him
this time.

At the end of the meeting, when Plymouth returned once
more to the problem of evacuating foreign combatants from
Spain, the Italian Ambassador's expression changed perceptibly,
and he at once declared that 'it was not the time to consider that
problem'.

1. The French word *'combattants'* is widely used in international legal
documents. It denotes persons belonging to the armed forces.

'And why is it not the time?' I asked in a very innocent tone.

'Because,' replied Grandi, 'the Committee should first resolve the more pressing questions involved in bringing the control plan which we have accepted into operation.'

'To my mind,' I retorted, 'there is nothing more pressing and important for us at the present time than the evacuation from Spain of the so-called "volunteers".'

Grandi began a long and rhetorical speech to prove that the 'volunteers' played a quite insignificant role in the Spanish war, and that the Soviet side was dragging up the matter purely for propaganda purposes. In doing so he got very worked up, and I noted to myself 'He's rising!' To add fuel to the flames, I began to 'stare out' the Italian Ambassador fixedly. He gave way first, stirred uneasily in his chair and tried to turn away. But I kept my eyes on him, and slowly, with pauses, putting deliberate emphasis on certain words, I asked: 'Are we to understand the Italian Ambassador as meaning that Italy and Germany, contrary to the decision of the Committee, are positively refusing to bring their "volunteers" out of Spain?'

And here Grandi's Italian temperament again did him a disservice. He, as it were, broke his chain, and suddenly fired out in one breath: 'If you want my opinion, I'll say this, not one single Italian volunteer will leave Spain until Franco is victorious!'

This was the very admission we had been trying to get. A very meaningful silence settled over the table of the Sub-committee. Then Plymouth began to put the arguments to Grandi, proving how essential it was to evacuate foreign combatants as soon as possible. Corbin came in to support Plymouth. Cartier suddenly awoke, disturbed by the raised voices, and started his customary enquiries: 'What's the matter? What are we speaking of?'

And Palmstierna exclaimed as if aside: 'Vileness and more vileness!'

The same day I told the journalists I knew what had happened in the Sub-committee. And the next morning the papers were full of the sensation: Italy refuses to withdraw her 'volunteers' from Spain. The perfidy of the Fascist powers, who had only just agreed to the control plan and to the evacuation of foreign combatants from the Pyrenean peninsula, was exposed to all the world. The campaign in support of the Spanish Republic sprang up with fresh strength.

On 24 March there was a plenary meeting of the Committee. Ribbentrop and Grandi created the usual scene at it about the 'leakage' of secret information to the press, but I remained utterly calm, as if the noise had nothing to do with me whatever, and it all ended once more in nothing.

Grandi's attempts outside of the Committee to refute the authenticity of the phrase which he had involuntarily let slip at the Sub-committee meeting on 23 March also met with failure: the Italian Ambassador could adduce no facts in support of his refutation. It was only after this that Plymouth, wishing to make some gesture at meeting Grandi halfway, proposed that short-hand notes should be taken not at plenary meetings of the Committee only, but in the Sub-committee as well. His proposal was accepted by the Sub-committee on 15 April 1937.

But let us return to the plenary meeting on 24 March. Not long before it, on 13 March to be precise, the Spanish Republican government had sent a Note to the European powers drawing their attention to the fact that, in contravention of the decision taken by the Committee prohibiting 'voluntary service', the Italian government was sending thousands of new 'volunteers' to help Franco. I received instructions from Moscow to raise this urgently in the Committee. Unfortunately Moscow was rather late in giving the instruction, and I was not able to bring forward a motion in strict conformity with the established rules of procedure. I had to 'grapple and board' Plymouth.

After the Committee had confirmed, almost without discussion, the principal staff appointments to the control organisation which the Committee had created, I remarked to the Chairman with my most innocent air: 'I would like to make a short statement.'

'What about?' enquired Plymouth nervously.

'The question concerns the subject under discussion,' I

answered, and at once began to set out the complaint against the unceasing despatch to Spain of Italian armed forces.

Plymouth tried to stop me, on the grounds that he had not been advised beforehand of my speech, but I went on speaking, taking no notice of his protests.

The Chairman whispered with his secretaries, and his face assumed the bewildered expression which it usually wore when the secretaries were giving him utterly conflicting advice. This gave me heart, and I completed my speech without further hindrance. It concluded with a specific proposal by the Soviet government: that representatives of the Committee be sent to Spain immediately to establish the justice or otherwise of the accusations made by the lawful government of the Spanish Republic against the Italian government.

I had barely finished when Grandi exploded. 'The provocatory statement made just now by the representative of Communist Russia,' he declared, 'will have from the Fascist government of Italy the answer it deserves!'

Ribbentrop and Monteiro supported their colleague. The rest stayed silent. Corbin came to the aid of the bewildered Chairman; he proposed that the Soviet statement be passed to the Sub-committee for consideration. No one objected.

At that stage the Easter holidays came along. The Committee and Sub-committee held no meetings for 3 weeks. The first meeting of the Sub-committee after Easter was not until 15 April, and at it Plymouth appealed to all its members 'to bring a spirit of goodwill to the solution of the problems with which the Committee is faced'. Grandi responded by declaring that he was prepared to consider once again the detailed plan for evacuation of foreign nationals from Spain.[1] So then I, with the agreement of the Soviet government, did not insist on consideration of the proposal made on 24 March.

The Fascist powers, however, continued to sabotage the control plan, and made use of a new device to do so; they with-

1. More will be said below about the reasons for this change of position by Italy.

held their payments towards the cost of the control organisation. Only a firm declaration by the u.s.s.r. that we would pay nothing until the other members of the Committee had paid in their share did something to get matters moving. Even after this, though, Ribbentrop still tried to gain time. He suddenly announced that in view of the paucity of Germany's reserves of foreign currency, she was going to pay her share in marks and in kind (in typewriters, office furniture, etc.). Even Plymouth felt this was too much. A long and acrimonious discussion started up on the German payments, which occupied many days before the matter was finally settled.

Then unexpected difficulties arose over appointing the staff of the control organisation. The reader already knows that, according to the decision taken by the Committee, the staff was to consist of nationals of all the states which were signatories to the Agreement on 'Non-intervention', in a fixed proportion. Up to 8 March Ribbentrop and Grandi were full of assurances that no difficulties were foreseen in this respect. Then all of a sudden it transpired that the Germans and Italians 'were not prepared', if you please, 'to serve abroad'. Again, much time was needed before this further unexpected obstacle was overcome.

The British and French treated the saboteurs with their usual tolerance. They looked sour, shrugged their shoulders, complained *sotto voce* of the intransigence of the Germans and Italians, but never once displayed the firmness that was needed. And if there had been no representative of the u.s.s.r. on the Committee, the control plan would in fact never have been brought into operation.

The longer it went on, the clearer became the real meaning of the farce enacted in London: in effect both groups, Germans and Italians *and* British and French, were engaging in intervention on Franco's side. The only difference was that Hitler and Mussolini did it with visor up, bare-faced, while the 'democratic' powers bashfully disguised it as 'non-intervention'.

This makes it clearer why the date for bringing the control plan into actual operation was systematically pushed farther and farther into the future. At the meeting on 8 March it was decided that the starting date was to be 13 March. This date came and went, but the control plan remained on paper only. Only on 19 April 1937 did the plan at last start to function on a limited scale, and only on 5 May did it take effect in its entirety. Thus almost two months had been wasted between the time of the plan's final ratification by the Committee and its coming into operation. This was a species of tribute which the 'appeasers' of London and Paris saw fit to pay to the Fascist aggressors, at the expense of the Spanish people.

I well remember the state of ecstasy into which the representatives of some 'democratic' powers fell, when in spite of everything the control plan began to come into operation. Palmstierna the Swede informed me that 'Public opinion is a great force, you see . . . Even Hitler and Mussolini are obliged to bow before it.'

Masaryk remarked: 'I am quite aware of all the weaknesses of Britain and France, but you must admit nevertheless that in this case they have acted energetically and carried their point. . . . Now German and Italian intervention will at least be very much reduced, even if it does not cease altogether.'

I was much more sceptically disposed; I expected new tricks from the Fascist powers, and remained constantly on the alert. The Soviet representatives on the Committee for 'Non-intervention' were not deceived as to the true reasons under pressure of which Germany and Italy had been obliged to agree to the control plan coming into operation.

The point was that on 26 April 1937 German aircraft disguised under Franco's colours had bombed to pieces a little town in the north of Spain called Guernica—an ancient centre of the Basque culture, a place entirely without military significance. The Fascist airmen did not content themselves with dropping their bombs from a height. They dived to roof-top level and machine-gunned the peaceful inhabitants of Guernica in their streets and gardens, on their farms and roads.

This savage slaughter of completely innocent people, women and children among them, evoked a storm of indignation through-

I

out the world. Even the Catholic church was alarmed, and some of its eminent figures came out with protests. Murmurings were heard even in London diplomatic circles. At the Sub-committee meeting on 4 May, Corbin, with Plymouth's support, put forward a proposal that the Committee approach 'both parties' in Spain with an appeal to refrain in future from bombing 'open cities'. The universal horror at the cruelty of the German air force (such things were still new then) compelled Hitler and Mussolini to manoeuvre. The Fascist dictators needed somehow to reassure world opinion, and they decided that this could best be done by their agreeing to bring the control plan, already accepted by the Committee, into operation.

The Fascist powers were all the more ready to make this small tactical concession since they were at that very time engaged in making important changes in their general plan for the war in Spain. After the defeat at Guadalajara Hitler and Mussolini at last began to realise that their aggression against Spain was assuming the character of a long-term operation. This was a great disappointment to them, but the facts could not be denied.

In the spring of 1937 the General Staffs of Germany and Italy worked out a new plan of operations in the Iberian peninsula. The first task, according to this plan, was the elimination of the northern front, that is the subjection of the Asturias and the Basque Country, which were part of the Spanish Republic. After that was to come the isolation of the Spanish Republic from France, that is the seizure of Catalonia or at least its northern provinces, adjacent to the French frontier.

Of course even the successful achievement of both these aims would not in itself guarantee the fall of the Spanish Republic. But there was no doubt that victory for the Fascists in the north and in Catalonia would make the position of the Spanish democrats much more difficult.

Politically speaking, the north of Spain presented a somewhat variegated picture. In the Asturias the dominant force was the revolutionary miners, among whom were many Communists and left-wing Socialists. In the Basque Country the decisive force was the conservative and Catholic Basque National Party, in which the big bourgeois and the priests played the leading part. As a result of this the People's Republican front was weaker in the north than in other parts of the country, and Franco took advantage of this more than once.

Geography was on the enemy's side too. The territory held by the Republican forces in the north of Spain was a long (about 400 kilometres) and narrow (not more than 50 kilometres) strip of land along the shores of the Bay of Biscay, completely cut off from the principal regions of the Republic. Communications between the Basque capital, Bilbao, and Madrid could be maintained only by air, and that at great risk, since the flights had to be made either over the provinces occupied by the enemy, or over the sea surrounding the Peninsula. This isolated situation of the Republican north played a fateful part in its subsequent fortunes.

At the very beginning of April 1937 Franco started an attack upon the Basque Country, and by 9 April was blockading Bilbao. On 26 April, as has already been mentioned, Guernica was bombed. The battalions of the Basque militia, reinforced by Asturian miners, put up a stubborn resistance to the rebels. But the weight of armaments was too heavily in Franco's favour (or, to be more precise, in favour of the Italian interventionists, who provided the main mass of troops attacking the Basque capital); and on 20 June 1937 the Fascists seized Bilbao.

At this critical moment the Basque government behaved with cowardice, and thereby, of course, made the Fascists' further advance much easier. On 26 August they occupied Santander without a fight, and two months later, after putting up a heroic resistance, the revolutionary Asturias also fell. The Republican front in the north had been eliminated.

So the first point in the new German and Italian plan of action for the Spanish war had been successfully operated; but things were not to go so easily when they attempted to operate the second point, that is, to capture Catalonia.

Their second point provided for two major actions: an antigovernment *coup* in Barcelona, and a landing of Fascist troops to the north of the city. It must be said without beating about the bush that the state of affairs obtaining in Catalonia was very favourable to such actions. Catalonia had always been something in the nature of a state within the state. In former centuries the Catalans had explained this as a matter of their special national characteristics.[1] Later the nationalist aspect was reinforced by the political; Catalonia became a stronghold of anarchism, which gradually evolved in the direction of anarcho-syndicalism. The main channel for the latter was the trade unions—the National Confederation of Labour—which in Catalonia numbered hundreds of thousands of members. In this province the Socialists were in an extremely weak position compared to the Anarcho-syndicalists.

At the very beginning of the war what was known as the United Socialist Party (a party of a Communist character) came into being in Catalonia, but its influence too was comparatively limited. First fiddle here, as before, was played by Anarcho-syndicalists, who by convictions and habit were opponents of a strong central power. Between Madrid and Barcelona—later between Valencia[2] and Barcelona—a struggle constantly went on. Barcelona did all it could to try to extend the limits of its independence, at the expense of the authority of the central government. In the end matters reached such a pitch that the *Generalidad* (Catalonian government) started to print its own money, and even set up its own Secretariat for Foreign Affairs.

The tension in Catalonia was heightened by the keen struggles among various groupings and tendencies within anarcho-syndicalism. During the critical days of the defence of Madrid, four representatives of the National Confederation of Labour

1. The nationalist principle played no small part here also in the years of the sixth Spanish revolution (1931–9), when the main bearer of this principle was the s.k.r.—a party of petty-bourgeois Left Republicans of Catalonian nationality.

2. In November 1936 the Republican government was evacuated to Valencia.

entered the central Republican government. This was a truly revolutionary step. But it was not to the taste of many among the Anarcho-syndicalists; many did not like such 'reconciliation' with the state. There were some very noisy groups which accused the anarchist Ministers of betraying the ideals of anarchy and demanded that an immediate start be made upon the 'social revolution'. These excessively fiery 'r-rr-revolutionaries' shaded off, through various groupings with barely discernible gradations of opinion, into what were known as the 'no-control elements' — a shady fringe of criminal, gangster hangers-on, who had always been the accompanying satellite of the anarchist movement, and who became especially numerous and aggressive in war conditions.

The Trotskyite party of 'united Marxists' (POUM), headed by Nin, also expanded its activity in Catalonia under the high patronage of the National Confederation of Labour. It too carried on a furious fight against the central government and against the Communist Party of Spain, employing the lowest tricks of demagogy. It is true that the influence of the POUM was in no way to be compared with that of the anarchists, but the Trotskyites made up for their lack of backing by the viciousness of their propaganda and the ingenuity of their sabotage.

Lastly, an element which found it easy to infiltrate the motley and disordered ranks of the anarchists and the Trotskyites was the hired agents of Fascism. To camouflage their espionage activities on Franco's behalf they shouted louder than anyone in support of Catalan 'nationhood', and were more malicious than any in their slanders on the central government of the Republic.

At the same time, the participation of representatives of the National Confederation of Labour in the central government and in the *Generalidad* made it possible for the Anarcho-syndicalists to take into their own hands some important organs of state power. In Barcelona, for instance, they in effect took upon themselves the functions of guardians of public order. True, the Republican *Guardias de Asalto* did exist there, but alongside it were numerous patrol committees and a coastguard militia, which consisted almost to a man of Anarcho-syndicalists. These organisations had at their disposal tanks, armoured cars and machine-guns.

Using their strength to advantage, the Anarcho-syndicalists forced the *Generalidad* to pass a number of measures which in the situation then existing were clearly a hindrance to the prosecution of the fight against Fascism. But even more disastrous were the actions which they carried through independently, the avowed object of which was the establishment forthwith of so-called 'libertarian Communism'. In the name of this last, forcible socialisation of property was carried out in the villages, down to the last chicken a peasant might own; mass discontent was provoked in consequence.

And what was the position of the central government *vis-à-vis* Catalonia? It was remarkable for its extreme inconsistency, and the main responsibility for this must be borne by Largo Caballero and his immediate entourage. In fact the Prime Minister did nothing to guide Catalonian affairs into any rational channel. He simply swam with the current, not wishing to quarrel with the Anarcho-syndicalists, whom he needed as a weapon to use against Communists.

The combined effect of all these factors was that at the end of April 1937 the time was ripe for a *putsch*, which duly broke out and which had extremely serious consequences.

It began on 25 April with the treacherous murder in a Barcelona suburb, by 'persons unknown', of the Communist R. Cortado, leader of the 'United Socialist Youth of Catalonia'. The head of the Barcelona police, Rodriguez Salas (a member of the United Socialist Party), responded by repressive measures against the Trotskyites and 'no-control elements'. The political atmosphere in the city rose to fever heat. At nights there were clashes in the streets between the *Guardias de Asalto* and 'unknown groups' of armed men. Talks between the Anarcho-syndicalists and the Socialists on the possibility of holding a joint First of May demonstration ended in a breach of relations. On 3 May numerous squads of Anarcho-syndicalists disarmed the *Guardias de Asalto* and began to make their way closer to the city centre. The coast-guard militia played a particularly active role here.

These *putsch* supporters seized the central telephone exchange, placed machine-guns in strategic positions on the roofs of houses, settled their snipers in secret hide-outs. Barricades sprang up on many streets and squares. The offices of the Anarcho-syndicalist trade unions were transformed into something like fortresses.

The insurgents demanded the resignation of the chief of police, Salas, and of the Catalonian Minister for Home Affairs, Aiguade. But the *Generalidad* refused the demand.

The next day, 4 May, the police barracks were attacked. Hand-grenades and dynamite were brought into play. Fierce fights were joined on the roof-tops. There were victims on both sides.

In the evening the Anarchist Ministers and members of the Executive of the National Confederation of Labour arrived in haste from Valencia. They spoke over the radio to their followers, appealing to them to cease fighting at once and lay down their arms. These appeals were repeated at regular intervals throughout the next two days, but had little effect. The passions inflamed by the Fascist *provocateurs* proved too strong.

The events in Barcelona caused alarm and confusion on the Aragon front, where the majority of the troops were Anarcho-syndicalists. Some units almost turned to march on Barcelona. Only with the greatest of difficulty could they be persuaded not to open the front to Franco.

In these grim days the *Generalidad*, in which the SKR dominated, revealed its complete incompetence. It had neither the forces nor the decision needed to deal with the Fascist-inspired *putsch*.

The central government was compelled to take a hand. On the morning of 7 May major groupings of Republican police were sent from Valencia to Catalonia. These were reinforced by some military units, withdrawn from the Jarama front. The first skirmishes between the insurgents and the governmental forces took place in Tarragona and Reusa. The former were dispersed with comparative ease, and Republican troops entered Barcelona by the evening of 7 May.

The Catalan *putsch* was over. 950 people had been killed, 3,000 wounded. In spite of the high casualty list, the *putsch* had been very short-lived and unsuccessful compared with the hopes the Fascists had pinned to it. The rebels and interventionists did not succeed in utilising it and seizing Catalonia for themselves.

But the events of 3–7 May were a grim warning to the Spanish Republic, to all the parties of the People's Front. The appropriate political conclusions had to be drawn. And drawn they were. On 16 May 1937, under the pressure of the Communist Party (supported by the majority of the Socialists and Left Republicans), the Caballero government resigned. On 17 May a new government was formed, headed by the Socialist Juan Negrín, who had previously been Minister of Finance.

The new government also had its shortcomings. Possibly the greatest mistake made in its formation was the appointment as Defence Minister of the right-wing Socialist Indalecio Prieto, who did not believe in the strength of the Republic and feared the creation of a really revolutionary army (the disastrous consequences of this appointment became fully apparent a year later). None the less, the Negrín government represented an undoubted step forward. Unlike Largo Caballero, the new Premier understood the vital need to co-operate with the Communist Party, and did not grieve unduly that the Anarcho-syndicalists refused to come into his cabinet. He boldly slashed the numbers of Ministers from 18 to 9. This made the government more compact and functional, and, most important, the ratio of Communists within it was considerably higher.

The new government of the Spanish Republic[1] proved much

1. The Negrín cabinet was made up as follows: Juan Negrín (Socialist) —Prime Minister and Minister of Finance; Indalecio Prieto (Socialist)— Minister of Defence; Julio Sugasagoitia (Socialist)—Minister of Home Affairs; Vicente Uribe (Communist)—Minister of Agriculture; Jesus Ernades (Communist—later a renegade)—Minister of Education and Health; José Jiral (Left Republican)—Minister of Foreign Affairs; Francisco Jiner de los Rios (Left Republican)—Minister of Public Works; Jaime Aiguade (S.K.R.)—Minister of Labour and of Social Insurance; Manuel Irujo (Basque Nationalist)—Minister of Justice.

more effective in the energetic prosecution of the war, and showed a stability unusual in those troubled times. With two partial changes (in April and August 1938) it continued in existence right up to the very end of the war, that is, almost two years.

The failure of the Catalan *putsch* and the formation of the Negrín government showed clearly that the Spanish Republic had come out of the May crisis not weakened but considerably strengthened. By the end of May there were no doubts left on that score in Rome or Berlin. The corollary was that if Franco was to win, then his armies would need further reinforcements of men and war materials, therefore Germany and Italy would be needing complete freedom of sea communications with Spain and Portugal. The control established by the Committee cramped these to some extent, and made extra expenditure necessary. So Hitler and Mussolini decided to finish the whole control system at one blow.

It was done like this. On 28 May 1937, at a plenary meeting of the Committee, Grandi made a strong protest against actions by the Republican air force. He alleged that on 24 and 26 May 5 Republican aeroplanes had raided Majorca (the largest of the Balearic Isles) and bombed the port of Palma, where Italian men-of-war and merchant vessels were at anchor, as also were vessels of other nations. Using his voice to great dramatic effect and emphasising his words with carefully worked-out gestures, Grandi exclaimed threateningly: 'The Fascist government reserve to themselves, and to themselves alone, the right to protect howsoever and wheresoever the Italian flag, as well as the lives and interests of their nationals. This is not the question which I am raising in the Committee.'

He then adopted a quieter tone and began to assert that the Italian warships alleged to have been the victims of attack from the air in Palma were carrying out duties as part of the sea patrols set up by the Committee. In this way the attack by Republican planes on Majorca, leading to the deaths of 6 officers of the Italian fleet, could be said to challenge the authority of the Committee.

'The Fascist government therefore expect,' declared Grandi, again assuming a dramatic tone, 'the Committee to reassert its authority and its prestige, seriously shaken by these acts, through which the Authorities of Valencia have challenged an International organ.'

The representatives of Germany and Portugal naturally hastened to support their Italian colleague once again. There was nothing unusual in that. What was less usual was the behaviour of the Committee's chairman. Plymouth was not at the meeting of 28 May; he had gone away for a fortnight on business of his own. His place was being temporarily filled by a Conservative politician, Euan Wallace. Plymouth was no hero, especially when it came to offering resistance to the Fascist powers, but he did at least have the ability to preserve a certain appearance of 'impartiality'. Euan Wallace, on the contrary, wanted to stress in every possible way that his sympathies were entirely on the side of Italy and Germany. He spoke immediately after Grandi and humbly bowed and scraped before the Italian Ambassador, and took the latter's every word as gospel truth. The acting Chairman of the Committee not only expressed 'deep regret' at the losses suffered by the Italian navy but proclaimed for all to hear: 'We shall protest at once and energetically to the Valencia Government against what we regard as an outrage.'

The very words 'Valencia Government' in the mouth of an official representative of Great Britain, a country maintaining normal diplomatic relations with the Spanish Republic, were highly symptomatic. They were the formula usually used by the representatives of the Fascist powers. But even more unnatural was the proposal to protest on the basis of Grandi's communication alone without hearing the explanation of the Spanish government. It all bespoke Wallace's burning desire to curry favour with the Fascist powers.

Corbin and Cartier displayed rather more *sang-froid* on this occasion, but they too supported the general line taken by Wallace. And the ever-thoughtful Hemming had already prepared a corresponding draft resolution, which might easily have been passed by the Committee if the Soviet side had not stood out against it.

I was not able to attend the meeting of 28 May in person owing to illness. A short time prior to this, during the coronation of George VI, I and all the rest of the *corps diplomatique* had had to take a sea trip. It was a sunny day, but a terrible wind was blowing; I got thoroughly chilled and went down with a severe attack of malaria. S. B. Kagan was deputising for me at the 28 May meeting, and he gave Wallace a very firm answer.

Kagan put the matter like this: it was not possible to pass any resolution on the basis of hearing one side only: one must hear the opinion of the other side, that is, of the Spanish government; the Italian Ambassador's statement that the Italian naval vessels which had been attacked were fulfilling naval control functions was incorrect—Palma was not within the zone allotted to Italy for patrolling.

A long and heated discussion arose between Kagan and the Fascists plus Wallace. The result was that Hemming had to do some serious rewriting of his draft resolution. The Committee resolved to request the Spanish government for explanations concerning the bombardment of Palma.

Three days later the Fascists produced another little surprise. A meeting of the Sub-committee had been fixed for the morning of 31 May. When all those assembled had taken their seats, it appeared that the places reserved for Germany and Italy were empty. The only one of the Fascists present was the Portuguese, Monteiro, and he, as it later transpired, had come only in order to be able to inform his 'elder brothers' of what happened.

Euan Wallace was in state of near-panic. He announced that a letter had been received from Ribbentrop, a letter of exceptional importance. At Wallace's request, Hemming read out this document aloud.

Ribbentrop wrote:

'On Saturday 29 May the armoured vessel *Deutschland* was peacefully at anchor in the roadstead of Ibiza [one of the Balearic Isles—I.M.]. Between 6 and 7 o'clock in the evening bombs were

suddenly dropped by two aeroplanes of the red Valencia authorities swooping down on the battleship ... 22 dead and 83 wounded
were the result of this assault ...

'This attack on the armoured vessel *Deutschland* belonging to
the International Sea Control, is the final link in a chain of
similar events. ...

'I am instructed by my Government to state the following on
their behalf:

'1. The German Government will discontinue to participate
in the control-scheme as well as in the discussions of the Non-
Intervention Committee as long as they have not received all
guarantees against the recurrence of such events ...

'2. In retaliation of the criminal assault of red bombing aeroplanes of the Valencia authorities on the armoured vessel *Deutschland* while at anchor, German vessels this morning shelled the
fortified port of Almeria. After the harbour-works had been
destroyed and the batteries of the opponents silenced, the act of
retaliation was terminated.'

When Hemming had finished reading Wallace added, anything but calmly, that he had been visited that morning by
Grandi, who had informed him of Italy's refusal to participate
further in the Committee for 'Non-intervention'.

A tense silence reigned over the green table. The representatives of the capitalist powers were completely unnerved. The
Committee should have been protesting at the savage shooting
down of hundreds of completely innocent men, women and
children in the peaceful town of Almeria. But their minds were on
quite other things. The diplomats of the so-called 'democratic'
countries were scared to death that the whole farce of 'non-
intervention' would now collapse like a house of cards. The
French Ambassador Corbin expressed their true feelings more
frankly than anyone else:

'I think in this matter one, perhaps our main, preoccupation
must be to save the work of this Committee, I might say the
existence of this Committee ...'

And the Belgian Ambassador Cartier, who had as usual

dropped off while Ribbentrop's letter was being read, first of all asked for this missive to be read through once again, and then, when that had been done, remarked very sagely: 'It will be necessary to elucidate what is meant by guarantees. . . .'

This determined the direction of the ensuing discussion. Wallace, Corbin, Cartier and Palmstierna considered, backwards, forwards and sideways, what 'guarantees' precisely the German government was demanding as the condition of its return to the Committee. The theme underlying all the contributions to the discussion was 'Ah, what can we do to pacify the Fascist tiger!'

It was a repulsive and disgusting spectacle.

Kagan spoke strongly against 'appeasing' the aggressors. Calling the bombardment of Almeria 'outrageous', he stressed that the German government had, without informing the Committee of its criminal intentions, 'taken upon itself the functions of prosecuting attorney, judge, and executioner, all combined in one'. The Soviet representative demanded that the Committee should at the very least express regret at the deaths of the innocent victims of this arbitrary action.

What a hope! Euan Wallace was simply horrified at such 'impertinence' towards the Fascist brigands. The same feelings filled the breasts of most of the other Committee members.

Looking for a way out of a 'ticklish' situation, Cartier remarked half-jokingly: 'I do not see very much what further use we have in sitting round this table, except to enjoy our pleasant company. . . .'

Euan Wallace breathed a sigh of relief and proposed 'that the Committee adjourn without passing any resolution'.

Then he, and Corbin, Palmstierna and several others with him, began to fall over themselves to argue that approaches should be made to the British and French governments, requesting them to remove the conflict which had arisen with the Fascist powers, 'through diplomatic channels'. Until this could be done, Wallace, with the obvious approval of the majority of those present, declared it to be undesirable for meetings of either the Committee or the Sub-committee to be called.

I I

A shameful deal

IT seemed as though the whole ill-fated campaign for 'non-intervention' had come to its natural end. Democratic circles in Britain, France and other countries breathed a sigh of relief. Since the bombing of Guernica and the barbarous shelling of Almeria it had become clear to many that unless the impudence of the Fascist powers met the resistance it deserved, and met it now, the future was fraught with the most disastrous consequences.

The Soviet Embassy in London brought into play every contact it had, and made use of every opportunity that arose, in order to get rid as quickly and as completely as possible of the Agreement and the Committee for 'Non-intervention', which had assumed such perverted forms. I myself and my closest helpers (particularly comrades Kagan and Stolyar) spent a week in interminable talks with journalists, parliamentarians, trade unionists, civil servants, and, lastly, members of the government and people very close to it. We were trying to show them that the original idea on which the Agreement on Non-intervention had been based had been completely distorted in practice, that the position of Germany and Italy absolutely precluded the possibility of real neutrality on the part of the Great Powers in the Spanish conflict, that in the situation as it existed the so-called 'neutrality' of the 'democratic' powers in fact meant intervention against Republican Spain. From this we drew the conclusion that advantage should be taken of the walk-out by Germany and Italy, and the Committee buried in the historical archives with the minimum of fuss and argument.

It should be said that our propaganda for this approach during the first week of June 1937 found a sympathetic response in many hearts and minds. It undoubtedly exerted an influence on public opinion in Britain, and had a sensible effect on the behaviour of the French government as well as that of the British, in that critical period.

It fell to my lot to carry on talks with the leadership of the Labour Party. For several days I was meeting and talking with its most prominent political figures, also with the leaders of the trade unions. The picture that emerged from all this was rather odd. Almost all those with whom I spoke agreed with me in principle, but as soon as the conversation turned to practical conclusions, somehow it always transpired that it was impossible to do anything. The politicians said 'We should be glad to demand an end to non-intervention, but you see the trade union people won't agree to it.' While the trade unionists in their turn indicated that it was the politicians' fault. 'We're prepared to bury non-intervention tomorrow if you like, but they can't make their minds up.' The key to guessing the meaning of this charade was provided for me by a not very prominent but more forthcoming Labour man of radical persuasions. 'Our leaders—both the political ones and the trade unionists—are too much under the influence of the government, and are nervous of coming out against it . . . Besides, they're mortally afraid of the Communists and don't want to support anything that they are demanding.'

Looking back now, I can state with complete conviction that it is the British Labour Party (whose example was followed by the French Socialists) which bears the chief responsibility for preventing the whole edifice of 'non-intervention' from collapsing immediately after the shelling of Almeria, and for keeping the shameful farce going for almost 2 more years.

Besides the Labour Party people, I tried to establish contact then with certain influential people in governmental circles. My reception here was cooler, but also franker; a negative attitude to our proposals was expressed quite openly, sometimes with reasons advanced for this which betrayed an utter lack of understanding of the nature of the historical processes involved, on the part of Britain's foremost public figures. In this respect my conversation with Lord Plymouth was especially revealing. It remains deeply stamped in my memory.

We met at a diplomatic reception. It was a chance meeting, and in consequence was largely free from the official constraint which usually accompanied my contacts with the Committee's Chairman within the walls of the Foreign Office. I took advantage of this happy chance in order to sound out Plymouth's real attitudes more thoroughly—these being, most likely, those of the British government also. I began by asking what was the news on 'non-intervention'. Plymouth replied that Britain and France were engaged in talks with Germany and Italy concerning the return of the latters' representatives to the Committee, and that he, Plymouth, hoped for a favourable outcome to those talks.

'It is a very difficult business,' complained Plymouth. 'You know yourself how obstinate and intransigent the German and Italian governments are . . . But I think that you and I will be meeting again round the Committee table before long.'

'I beg your pardon, Lord Plymouth,' I interrupted. 'We are after all speaking privately just now . . . So I don't mind telling you plainly that I cannot understand why the British government is so attached to this Committee. After 9 months' experience of it I should have thought that it was clear to everyone that the Committee for "Non-intervention", in spite of the good intentions of those who began it, has in practice proved an absolutely unsuitable method for limiting the war in Spain to the Spaniards themselves.'

'Still, you will not try to deny,' objected Plymouth, 'that with all its faults, which I am very conscious of, our Committee has in these 9 months considerably reduced the danger of a European war starting . . .'

Plymouth flapped his dinner-jacket, which hung too loose on him, and added sadly: 'You see? . . . I've lost almost two stone in those 9 months. But I am consoled by the thought that that is my sacrifice on the altar of peace in Europe.'

'I should not like to disillusion you, Lord Plymouth,' I

remarked, 'but I must admit that from my point of view the Committee for "Non-intervention" has not diminished the danger of war in Europe, on the contrary it has increased it.'

'How can it have done that?' asked Plymouth in surprise.

'Very simply. . . . The Committee for "Non-intervention" has become a screen hiding the powerful support that Franco is getting from the Fascist powers. Those powers have sensed that they have no need to fear serious opposition to their plans for aggression—opposition in deeds, that is, not words—from Britain, France and the U.S.A. I am afraid that experience of this sort may confirm Hitler and Mussolini in their belief that they can escape retribution for any sort of provocation, however monstrous, in the international field. And if that is so, then the danger of war in Europe, perhaps even of another world war, has grown greater.'

Plymouth shrugged his shoulders and remarked with a superior smile: 'You are too much of a pessimist.'

'Alas, Lord Plymouth,' I replied, 'our Soviet pessimism, so far as the intentions and actions of the Fascist aggressors are concerned, has so far, unfortunately, always proved justified. . . . And, forgive me once more, I simply cannot understand your indifference to the future of the Iberian peninsula. . . . Let us leave aside for the minute the general interests of peace and European security. Let us pass on to viewing the question from what I would see as the very realist standpoint of Britain's own private, national interests. . . . Let us suppose that Franco is victorious in Spain, and that Germany gets a firm foothold in Spain. What will happen then to your British capital investments in that country? They are quite considerable, after all. . . . What will happen to your sea communications with the East, with Hitler threatening them? . . . What will happen to France, with the German threat closing in, front and rear? . . . How can you British reconcile yourselves to such prospects? And I see no others, if the Committee for "Non-intervention" continues its ill-fated work. . . .'

Plymouth heard me out dispassionately, and then began an unhurried exposition of his *credo*:

K

'I must repeat—you are too much of a pessimist. . . . Our British interests are not threatened by serious danger even if Franco should win. . . . However the war ends, Spain will come out of it completely ruined. She will need money to restore her economy. . . . And where is she to get it from? Not from Germany and Italy, anyway; they have no money. A devastated Spain can get money only in London. Whoever leads Spain after this war, he will have to come to our banks. . . . That is when our hour comes. . . . We shall be able to come to terms with the future government of Spain on all the things that interest us: financial compensation, and political and military guarantees as well. . . . No, our interests will not suffer, whatever the outcome of the war may be!'

I listened and could not help but wonder at the *naïveté* of this man, who, as it were, personified the ruling class of Great Britain. Plymouth was in thrall to the traditions and views of the 19th century; he was unable to grasp the mechanics of economic and political relations in our age. However, I did not start explaining the difference between 'then' and 'now' to Lord Plymouth, I simply said: 'You called me too great a pessimist. . . . After listening to you, I am inclined to think that you are over-confident. . . . History will soon show which of us is right, and which wrong.'

History did indeed show, and much sooner than I expected. After his victory Franco did not come to bow down to the Golden Calf in the City. He remained a German puppet up to the very end of the Third Reich, and then quickly transferred his allegiance to the u.s.a. Britain and France lost their former influence in Spain. . . . That was the price they paid for their policy of 'non-intervention'.

Let us return, however, to 1937.

The illusions of Britain's ruling circles, which came out so clearly in my conversation with Plymouth, were reinforced by certain political events of an all-European nature.

On 28 May 1937 Britain's Prime Minister Baldwin retired, and his place as head of the government was taken by Neville

Chamberlain—the leader of the so-called 'Cliveden set', which brought together the most reactionary groups of the British bourgeoisie. On 25 June he spoke in Parliament; it was a major policy statement, in which he depicted the existing international situation in the blackest colours.

'. . . in the high mountains there are sometimes conditions to be found when an incautious move or even a sudden loud exclamation may start an avalanche. That is just the condition in which we are finding ourselves today . . . if we can all exercise caution, patience and self-restraint we may yet be able to save the peace of Europe . . . let us try to keep cool heads and neither say nor do anything to precipitate a disaster . . .'[1]

Lloyd George, who spoke after Chamberlain, remarked—not altogether without malice—that '. . . any fish can have a cool head', but that rather more was needed if a way out of the international blind alley was to be found: here '. . . we must have not only cool heads but stout hearts'. And this was just what was lacking in the Chamberlain government, the result being that as from June 1937 Britain openly slid down the slope of disgraceful, criminal deals with the Fascist aggressors, who 26 months later flung her into the second world war.

This general line of the new British cabinet affected the attitude taken on Spain also. It caused a further intensification of the 'non-intervention' policy.

France appeared in no more impressive a role. On 20 June the Blum government fell, and was succeeded by the Chautemps government, in which the 'appeasers' really played first fiddle. Suffice it to say that a sinister figure like Bonnet appeared as one of its Ministers.

A touching solicitude for the maintenance of the 'non-intervention' farce was evinced on the other side of the ocean, too. I have already related how the American government had from the very beginning given its blessing to Britain and France in this inglorious cause. Later the Washington politicians went even

1. Parliamentary Debates, Commons, vol. 325.

further: though not bound by any Agreement on Non-intervention, they quite voluntarily and on their own initiative refused to sell arms to the Spanish Republic. More: Washington stepped up the pressure on Mexico, forbidding her to offer for re-sale to the Spanish democrats arms bought in the u.s.a.

The State Department displayed a simply shameful state of nervousness when Ribbentrop and Grandi declared they were leaving the Committee for 'Non-intervention'. By 1 June, that is the day following the halt called in the Committee's work Bingham, the American Ambassador in London, was already calling on Eden, the Foreign Secretary, and informing him that the u.s.a. was 'concerned at the situation that had arisen' and would like to know how the British government proposed to conduct itself. The very tone of Bingham's proceedings made it easy to judge that the State Department considered it exceptionally important to restore the Committee for 'Non-intervention' as quickly as possible.[1]

The following almost comic incident provides a striking illustration of the extremes to which American politicians took the principle of 'non-intervention'.

In the spring of 1937, just before the fall of Bilbao, several thousand Spanish children were evacuated from the Basque Country and the Asturias, by their parents' wish, to other European countries (the u.s.s.r., Britain, France); a small proportion were sent to Mexico. On 5 June the ship brought 500 small Spanish citizens in to New York, from whence they were to proceed by land across the Mexican border. What, it might have seemed, could be more innocent or more natural? But no! The American authorities decided otherwise. In their imagination the 500 small children took on the terrible aspect of 500 combatants from one of the warring sides in the Spanish conflict. And so the children were not allowed to land. . . .

It is hardly surprising that with a background of this sort the

1. *The Foreign Relations of the U.S.A. Diplomatic papers 1937.* Washington, 1954, vol. 1, p. 317. In the subsequent text these will be denoted as *American Documents.*

governments of Britain and France began humbly to beg the Fascist powers to relent the very minute Germany and Italy had left the Committee and the naval patrols had ceased to function. Now many documents have been published which illumine all the details of the talks among the 4 powers mentioned above after the shelling of Almeria. Comparing these with what came to my knowledge in various ways concerning these talks at the time, in June 1937, I discover to my satisfaction that the Soviet Embassy in London had sufficiently reliable information at its command. All the basic and essential points we knew; all that was lacking were some of the particular finishing touches—sometimes very colourful ones.

As soon as 2 June 1937, according to the afore-mentioned Bingham,[1] the British government sent instructions to its Ambassadors in Rome and Berlin to propose to the governments of Germany and Italy joint discussions with Britain on a programme of measures which would satisfy the Fascist powers. In practice this meant giving concrete form to the 'guarantees' demanded by Ribbentrop in his Note to the Committee of 31 May. In the opinion of the British government such guarantees might be summarised as follows:

1. Firm declarations by 'both parties' in Spain, that they would from now on maintain a non-hostile attitude not only towards naval vessels carrying out naval control functions, but towards all naval vessels without qualification, while the latter should be in Spanish waters.

2. Precise enumeration of the Spanish ports on which naval patrol vessels were to be based, and the establishment in these ports of special 'safety zones', not liable to air attack.

3. Warning to be given to 'both parties' in Spain that any violation by them of the undertakings given would be considered by all the four powers together in joint consultation on the situation thus created.[2]

This was not enough for the Fascist powers. In a telegram

1. *American Documents*, vol. 1, p. 322.
2. *American Documents*, vol. 1, p. 325.

dated 7 June 1937 the American Ambassador in Rome, Phillips, informed Washington that 'Italy and Germany have approved in principle the proposals made [by the British—I.M.] but are asking for the third point to be made stronger, since they consider it to be too weak, by giving each power which has suffered attack the right to take appropriate measures independently, without consultation with the other three powers'.[1]

The British hastened to yield to the Fascist pressure, and accepted their correction on the third point. After that Eden conferred with the German, Italian and French Ambassadors, and settled the final formulation of all the details of an Agreement dated 12 June 1937.[2]

It was indeed a shameful deal. The Fascists were given the right to maintain their naval vessels in Spanish waters, not only for patrol purposes, but for assisting the rebels also. The Fascists kept their hands free so that at any moment they could repeat a performance such as Almeria. The Fascists, further, got the support of Britain and France in the case of any conflicts with the Spanish Republic. It was a little Munich, a dress rehearsal for the big one.

Of course, in return for such a 'gold nugget the size of a horse's head' Germany and Italy were prepared to make a small concession, and on 18 June Ribbentrop and Grandi made their appearance at the first meeting of the Sub-committee since the adjournment.

This meeting was of no great importance in itself: an extremely academic point, that of the 'humanisation of war', was the matter under discussion. As far back as 4 May, under the direct impact of the bombardment of Guernica, the British and French had tabled a proposal that an appeal be made to Franco and the Spanish government to refrain from aerial bombardment of open cities. As things then stood this proposal could not have had any serious

1. Ibid., vol. 1, p. 326.
2. *Documents on German Foreign Policy 1918–1945*, London, 1951. Series D, vol. III, p. 327. Communication from the first deputy of the German Ambassador in London, 12.VI.37.

significance, but it did at least have a clear and limited object, and the fulfilment or non-fulfilment of obligations by the two sides could be checked with comparative ease; for this reason the Fascists, especially Ribbentrop, did not like it.

To come out directly against the Anglo-French proposal was awkward. The representatives of Germany and Italy repeated their old, their favourite, trick; they did their best to drown the real matter in a sea of vague aspirations. At every meeting the Fascists produced from some inexhaustible secret store more and more 'forms of cruelty' involved in war, and insisted on their being mentioned in the appeal. In the end the latter came to resemble a litany, very righteous but entirely without practical significance. There were no grounds for objecting to it, but likewise no grounds for going into ecstasies over it. And it was this document, utterly castrated, bloodless and like to an anaemic plant, that Plymouth produced for the Sub-committee to decide on at the 18 June meeting. The document was accepted almost without discussion. The meeting lasted not more than half an hour. But it was very necessary to Plymouth, very necessary to the British and French governments, as a demonstration that the recent quarrel with the Fascist powers had been ended.

The press loudly advertised the Sub-committee's meeting. But broad democratic opinion in Britain, France and other countries expressed deep disgust at the agreement reached. Fierce protests against the actions of the 'appeasers' began to make themselves heard. The result was that Chamberlain and Blum had to take to manœuvring again.

When a few days later the Nazis raised a terrible noise over a fresh 'incident', this time involving the German cruiser *Leipzig* (which was supposed to have been attacked on 15 and 18 June by some mysterious submarines), there was a clash between the British and French on the one side and the Germans and Italians on the other. Germany, supported by Italy, demanded an immediate demonstration at sea by all four powers together against the Republican government, but in the situation then obtaining Chamberlain and Blum did not dare go so far as this.

The British declared that first of all the incident must be carefully investigated. The French held that there was no convincing proof of the guilt of the Republican government of Spain, and that if there was to be any demonstration of protest, then it should be made to include Franco also. This the Germans and Italians could not accept.

There was a moment when in both London and Paris they expected another Almeria. But the storm which the first Almeria had raised throughout the world obliged Hitler and Mussolini to behave a little more cautiously this time. Germany and Italy confined themselves to refusing finally, on 23 June, to take any further part in naval patrolling . . . but meantime remaining members of the Committee for 'Non-intervention'. The sense of this tactic was easy to follow: it was the patrols at sea which caused the most inconvenience to the Fascist powers, so they decided to wreck them, whereas the existence of the London Committee did most to aggravate the position of the Spanish Republic, so the Fascist powers did their best to preserve this still-born creature.

The 'manœuvres' of the British and French came into play over another issue too. In the middle of May the Committee's experts had worked out a plan for the evacuation of foreign combatants from Spain, and this had been sent to all the governments which had signed the Agreement on 'Non-intervention', for their conclusions. Germany and Italy were still 'studying' it. And the British government decided to take advantage of this circumstance in order to raise its own political stock, at least slightly, in the eyes of world public opinion. At the meeting of the Sub-committee on 21 June Plymouth made a speech full of feeling:

'His Majesty's Government feel the keenest disappointment that, in spite of the agreements entered into and the elaborate organisations set up, arms and war material continue to reach both sides in Spain . . .'

It was further noted in Plymouth's speech that '. . . the presence of large numbers of foreign nationals in Spain is one of the most unsatisfactory features of the present situation'. And inasmuch as certain governments were delaying their reply to the scheme elaborated by the Committee for the evacuation of these combatants from the Iberian peninsula, Britain recommended that a step, even if only a symbolic one, in this direction should be taken at once. In concrete terms, Plymouth proposed an approach to both sides in Spain, requesting their agreement to the evacuation of a small number of such volunteers, the same number in each case. The first step was always the hardest. If this were taken, it would be easier to carry through the general plan for such an evacuation, with all the necessary guarantees and proportions observed.

The sense of Plymouth's proposal was clear: if this was successfully carried through, the 'appeasers' would have raised a terrific noise about 'the first practical step' having been taken, thus proving that the Agreement on 'Non-intervention' was useful, and that they had not been wasting time in working for its resurrection.

It was on this account that the Soviet side came out firmly against the British proposal.

'. . . roughly the total number of foreigners fighting on the side of General Franco is 100,000, and, on the other hand, at the outside, the present number of foreign fighting forces with the Spanish Government is not more than 15,000 or 18,000 at the most. If you were to evacuate 5,000 from one side and 5,000 from the other side, what would it mean? General Franco would lose only 5 per cent of his foreign troops, but the Spanish Government would lose something like one-third. . . . Would this be just or fair? I do not think so.'

The Soviet side succeeded in making Plymouth's motion go down, and the British and French lost their opportunity of throwing dust in the eyes of world public opinion.

The final refusal of Germany and Italy to participate in naval control, mentioned above, was a heavy blow at the whole control plan, for its different parts were closely interlinked. The loss of one link, naturally, threw out the whole delicately balanced mechanism. After all, if naval patrolling ceased, control at sea in fact ceased to be effective. And if control at sea ceased, then control of Spain's land frontiers lost all meaning, and, consequently, exactly nothing of the control plan was left.

These considerations occasioned great worry to the British and French, who wanted to continue their criminal game at all costs. In order to find a way out of a ticklish situation, Plymouth and Corbin at the Sub-committee meeting of 29 June declared on behalf of their governments that they were prepared to maintain naval patrolling of the entire Spanish coast with the forces of the British and French fleets alone, but that it must be with 'neutral observers' present on board their ships.

The representatives of Belgium, Sweden and Czechoslovakia supported the British and French. I too, on behalf of the Soviet Union, supported the maintenance of naval patrolling in its new form. But Ribbentrop and Grandi attacked the Anglo-French proposal outright, affirming that the scheme of control at sea provided for in the plan of 8 March had proved an entire failure and could not be revived. At the same time both Fascist representatives hinted vaguely that control at sea should in future be based on quite different principles. I asked Ribbentrop to indicate more precisely the nature of these new principles. But the German Ambassador declined to give a direct answer.

The mystery was resolved only at the next meeting of the Sub-committee, on 2 July. This time Ribbentrop made a concrete proposal, in the name of the German and the Italian governments, the main points of which were as follows:

1. Control by land to remain in its previous form.

2. Instead of control by sea in its old form, 'both parties' in Spain to be considered as having the rights of belligerents. Each of them might set up a sea blockade of the enemy, i.e. seize in the open sea all vessels of any nationality bound for enemy ports, and might confiscate their cargoes under so-called 'prize right'.

Plymouth, Corbin and the other representatives of the 'democratic' powers gave the German and Italian proposal a rather ill-defined reception. The French Ambassador even spoke against it, but in a very mild and somewhat ambiguous way. As for me, I began at once to object quite categorically.

In the last resort a decision was taken to consult all the governments on their attitude to the German and Italian proposals. General discussion of the latter was transferred to the plenary meeting of the Committee.

There was such a meeting on 9 July. At it Plymouth and Corbin continued to defend their plan, and Ribbentrop and Grandi did the same. The majority of representatives of other powers were vague as to where they stood, and spoke to the effect that some middle way should be found. On this occasion also I spoke in sharp criticism of the Fascist proposals.

'. . . the considered view of the Soviet Government,' I said, '[is] that complete naval control off the Spanish coasts is an essential element of the Non-intervention Scheme, and without it the very basis on which the non-intervention was built up . . . must inevitably go. The granting of belligerent rights to General Franco is a very complicated problem which raises the gravest issues.

'In the first place, this problem must be considered in its legal aspect. To grant belligerent rights to General Franco would mean putting the legitimate Government of the Spanish Republic and the rebellious General who, in defiance of his oath, took up arms against his Government, on the same legal basis. Such an action would obviously be contrary to international law, international custom and tradition, and consequently cannot be accepted . . . In the second place, the German-Italian proposals should also be considered from the military point of view, as to their effect on the course of the Spanish war . . .'

After going on to note that the Spanish conflict had long since lost the character of a purely internal struggle, and enumerating a long list of facts showing the many forms of very effective aid which Franco was continually receiving from Germany and Italy, I continued:

'It is useless to try, as the German Representative tried at the last meeting of the Sub-committee, to quote the respective figures concerning the Republican fleet and the fleet of General Franco. The Spanish navy, in the event of belligerent rights being granted to General Franco, will be confronted not by the few obsolete vessels in the hands of the rebels, but also by the most modern naval forces of General Franco's foreign allies.

'. . . In practice the granting of belligerent rights would result in a complete and effective blockade of the Republican coast and in the utter impossibility of the Spanish Government instituting a similar blockade of the coasts in the hands of General Franco . . .'

In conclusion I repeated once again, in the name of the Soviet government, our positive attitude to the British and French plan put forward on 29 June.

Then the Polish Ambassador, Raczyński, made an emotional speech about the importance of maintaining the policy of non-intervention, and how 'foolish and even almost impermissible it would be to abandon the attempt to reach an agreement dictated by the spirit of compromise'. The Pole was supported by the representatives of Roumania, Yugoslavia, Greece, Austria, Turkey and other states. All of them insistently demanded a compromise.

In summing up the debate, Plymouth declared that His Majesty's government was ready to study sympathetically any proposals which might be of more assistance in overcoming the difficulties that have arisen than those proposals put before the Committee already.

Then the representative of the Netherlands, their Envoy van Swinderen, rose to his feet and proposed, in phrases of the most excessive elegance, that the British government, as represented in particular by the Committee's Chairman, Lord Plymouth, should be entrusted with the commission of drawing up a new, compromise plan, which would be a bridge between the Anglo-French and Italo-German plans. After this the following scene, which might almost have come from Gogol's pen, unfolded:

Lord Plymouth: Of course, Excellencies and Gentlemen, you have heard what the Netherlands Minister has said, but I should like an expression of views on the part of members of the Committee as to whether they think his suggestion is one that can be adopted in the circumstances.

Count Grandi: I support the suggestion made by the Netherlands Representative.

Charles Corbin: I am quite ready to agree to the suggestion made by the Netherlands Minister, which is according to the views I have expressed this morning.

Jan Masaryk: I want to associate myself with what the French Ambassador has said.

Joachim Ribbentrop: I support the words of the Netherlands Minister.

B. Grigorcea (Roumania): I do the same.

Bay Seki Örs (Turkey): I do the same.

A. Monteiro (Portugal): I am very happy to associate myself with the proposal of the Netherlands Minister. I think it is wisdom itself.

E. Raczyński (Poland): I also wish to support the proposal that has been made, that this very difficult task should be laid in your hands.

Baron de Cartier: I thoroughly approve of the wise suggestion of my Netherlands colleague.

V. Milanovitch (Yugoslavia): I desire to support the proposal of the Netherlands Minister.

E. Colban (Norway): I also wish to support my Netherlands colleague's proposal.

C. Simopoulos (Greece): I wish to do the same.

K. Zarin (Latvia): I also support the proposal of the Netherlands Minister.

Lord Plymouth: Excellencies and Gentlemen, if, as I understand, it is the unanimous desire of the Committee that His Majesty's Government should undertake the task of finding a way out of our difficulties, I am, of course, prepared to put that suggestion and that expression of the desire of the Committee before my Government . . .

.   .   .   .   .

Thus it was that matters drew close to the birth of the second control plan, which later came to be known as 'the British plan'.

The Soviet side did not raise any objection to the attempt to find a compromise solution, but I did consider it necessary to stress that 'the gulf between the two plans is too great, and it is scarcely possible to build a bridge between them which will be acceptable to all parties'.

My supposition proved to be correct.

12

The second control plan

A COMPROMISE control plan was laid before the Committee by Plymouth on 14 July 1937. In essence it was as follows:

1. Naval patrolling of the Spanish coast was to cease, but the Committee's observing officers would continue to be carried on board ships bound for Spanish ports. In the ports, by agreement with the Spanish government and with Franco, groups of observers from the Committee would be established, whose duty it would be to see that there were observing officers aboard all ships being unloaded.

2. Land control along the Franco-Spanish and Portuguese-Spanish frontiers to be immediately re-established in the form in which it was operating previously.

3. The government of the Spanish Republic, and Franco, each to be accorded belligerents' rights in a limited form, under condition of the evacuation of all foreign combatants from Spain.

4. Belligerents' rights to be recognised and come into force only after the London Committee for 'Non-intervention' had satisfied itself that 'substantial progress' had been made in the evacuation of foreign combatants.

The new plan underwent preliminary discussion in the Committee on 16 July 1937. All the members of the Committee agreed to accept it as a basis, but even at this meeting I made the following qualificatory remark: 'The British proposals require certain important modifications, which will be put forward by the Soviet government at a later stage.'

Plymouth was very pleased with the unanimous decision of

the plenary meeting, and in feeling words expressed his gratitude to all its members for the 'spirit of goodwill' they had shown. However, this idyll did not last long.

The British plan had an obvious bias in the direction of the Fascist powers' pretensions. In essence it eliminated the undesirable (to Germany and Italy) sea patrols, meant immediate closure of the Franco-Spanish border, which was a stab in the back for the Spanish Republic, put the government of Spain and the rebel General Franco on the same footing, promised both sides in the conflict recognition of belligerent's status in return for no more than 'substantial progress' in the evacuation of foreign combatants (and it remained quite unclear how in practice this vague formula of 'substantial progress' was going to be interpreted). It is not surprising that Ribbentrop and Grandi warmly welcomed such a plan, and if there had been no u.s.s.r. on the Committee there is no doubt but that this plan would have been speedily put into operation after being made somewhat worse in the course of discussion. Only the firm stand of the Soviet government nipped in the bud this grim, even mortal, threat to the Republic, and made the receipt of arms from abroad somewhat easier for that Republic's lawful government, for almost a whole year more.

At the meeting of the Sub-committee on 20 July, I made a statement, on the instructions of the Soviet government, that belligerent status could not be accorded to the parties to the war in Spain until such time as a satisfactory solution be found to the problem of the so-called 'volunteers', and that the success or failure of the whole British plan depended entirely on a favourable solution being found to this particular problem. We proposed that attention should be concentrated on settlement of the question of evacuating the foreign combatants from Spain, and only in the event of agreement being reached on this should the Committee go on to discuss the other points of the British plan. Furthermore, the Soviet government greatly doubted—and I adduced good reason for these doubts in the course of subsequent discussion—whether the Committee for 'Non-intervention' was competent to accord belligerent status to anyone at all.

The representatives of Germany and Italy were, contrariwise, of the opinion that in the first place attention should be given to that part of the British plan which concerned the accordance to 'both parties' in Spain of the rights of belligerents; that a decision should be taken on this first of all, and the question of the evacuation of the 'volunteers' left until later. In practice this meant that the Fascist powers, having succeeded in getting Franco accorded belligerent status, with the acquiescence of the British and French, would then have put the brake on the evacuation of foreign combatants from Spain until the war was over. At that same meeting of the Sub-committee, on 20 July, Ribbentrop let the cat out of the bag himself, proclaiming for all to hear:

'My government is, however, of the opinion that the granting of the rights of belligerency to the two parties in Spain should be put into effect at the earliest possible moment, and should not be unduly held up by any considerations with regard to the carrying out of the withdrawal of volunteers.'

Grandi was no less frank. 'In the opinion of the Italian government,' he declared, 'recognition of belligerent rights cannot be made subordinate to the withdrawal of volunteers, and must precede any provision whatsoever of that kind the Committee might eventually agree upon.'

As we see, there were two diametrically opposed points of view represented, between which it was impossible or at least very difficult to establish any saving link. This was so obvious that even Corbin did not consider it possible to seek a compromise, and supported the Soviet point of view. In the name of the French government he recognised the presence of foreign combatants in Spain to be 'the most important problem of the present situation' and proposed that it be discussed in the first place. Corbin's position undoubtedly reflected the deep indignation then felt by the broad masses of French democratic opinion, which demanded an end to the farce of 'non-intervention'.

Plymouth tried to take up an 'impartial' attitude, and spent a

L

lot of time trying to demonstrate that the British plan was con-
structed on the principle of interdependence of parts. But the
Chairman's arguments convinced no one, and the talks on the
new control plan ran into deadlock at the start.

Looking for a way to break this deadlock, Plymouth proposed
that the Committee's members should again consult their
governments on their attitude to the British plan and the order of
its discussion. The Sub-committee met on 30 July to consider
the answers received. At this meeting Ribbentrop, supported by
Grandi, fiercely attacked me, asserting that the position of the
u.s.s.r. was dealing a death-blow to the whole plan.

'The reason for this attitude on the part of Soviet Russia to us
is clear,' trumpeted the German Ambassador. 'Soviet Russia
started the Spanish Civil War and would like to end it in her
own way, that is by Bolshevising Spain.'

Naturally I administered a suitable rebuke, and then stressed
once again, with all the emphasis at my command, the first-rank
importance of the 'volunteers' problem:

'. . . what we have heard from their [Germany's and Italy's—
translator] representatives in the Committee for the last few weeks
makes us suspect that both these Governments are either definitely
opposed to the withdrawal or are trying to postpone it to an
indefinite future.'

In summing up the meeting of 30 July, Plymouth declared
that the future of the British plan depended upon a clear answer
being received to two questions: was the Soviet government
prepared to accord belligerent rights at all to 'both parties' in
Spain, and if it was prepared to do so, on what conditions? And
were the governments of Germany, Italy and Portugal prepared
to make the accordance of belligerent rights dependent upon the
successful settlement of the question of evacuation of 'volunteers'?

Plymouth again asked the representatives of these powers to
get in urgent touch with their governments.

At the next meeting of the Sub-committee, on 6 August, I
announced the answer of the Soviet government. It amounted
to this: for reasons of a juridical and political nature the Soviet

government had every ground for refusing to consider the question of accordance of belligerent status on any conditions; however, it attributed great significance to the effective realisation of non-intervention and wished to assist the work of the Committee, and therefore admitted the possibility of discussion of this question at a later stage, in the hope that in the last resort a satisfactory solution might be found to it. But we followed this with an immediate qualification, that the essential pre-condition for this was the favourable settlement of the problem of the 'volunteers'.

The U.S.S.R. thus went halfway to meet Plymouth and the British government. Well, and what of the Fascist powers? On 6 August their representatives did not open their mouths. Then I decided to repeat the manœuvre which had served me so well at the Sub-committee's meeting of 23 March 1937—I put the question point-blank to Woermann (who was deputising for Ribbentrop at this meeting): would they agree, without any qualifications, to the evacuation of foreign combatants from the forward line at once and subsequently from Spain itself, within a short time to be precisely fixed by the Committee?

Visible confusion appeared among the representatives of the Fascist powers. Then Woermann remarked, rather helplessly: 'Nothing is changed by the statement of the Soviet Ambassador and nothing could be changed by his questions to the individual representatives.'

This time Grandi also kept himself well in hand. He merely 'supported the views of the German representative'.

Then I summed up: 'After the short discussion we have had this afternoon I am justified in stating that the representatives of these three powers refuse to give a straight and definite answer to my straight and definite question. Such an attitude is in itself also an answer.'

The deadlock remained as complete as before.

Plymouth recognised this and decided to adjourn the discussion of the British plan until a more favourable moment, especially since the Parliamentary 'school holidays' had begun in Britain, during which time all self-respecting British politicians depart for the resorts and their own estates.

The pause in the activity of the Committee and Sub-committee lasted almost two and a half months.

In the meantime some important events took place.

First, the French government had found itself obliged, under the pressure of democratic circles in the country, to open the frontier between France and Spain completely from the middle of July 1937 until such time as the discussions of the British plan should be concluded in the Committee for 'Non-intervention'. And since that discussion dragged on until 5 July 1938 (which we shall consider in greater detail below), for eleven and a half months the Spanish Republic was able to receive arms through France. True, not everything here was plain sailing; the representatives of the '200 families', who found their way into every pore of the country's political and administrative body, thrust their spokes at every turn into the wheel of supply of war materials to the Spanish Republic. To this was added incredible corruption within the whole French apparatus of state, constant squabbling among the various parties and groups, rivalry between political cheapjacks, a venial press, and intrigues by the numerous right-wing organisations. Under such conditions every military cargo sent from Le Havre or Cherbourg to Spain was an absolute lottery, which you might win but might equally well lose. None the less, by making free use of a system of bribes to persons on whom depended the granting of passes for transport of arms across France, the Spanish government succeeded in replenishing its arsenals considerably during the winter of 1937–8.

Secondly, in view of the refusal of Germany and Italy to participate in patrols at sea, the British and French governments also ceased patrolling the Spanish coast, on 16 September 1937. Thus the two main pillars of the whole control system collapsed, and in effect all that was left of the plan accepted by the Committee on 8 March 1937 was 'horns and hoofs'. The U.S.S.R. drew the logical conclusion and declared that it would not continue to make the monetary payments towards the upkeep of the control system.

Thirdly, and lastly, in September 1937 the Conference of Nyons took place, which related directly to Spanish affairs. In their determination to hinder the Spanish Republic from getting supplies by sea, the rebels had made wide use of piracy in the Mediterranean and the Atlantic, with the energetic support of the Fascist powers (especially Italy). At first their attacks were directed principally against Soviet vessels. As far back as 11 November 1936, the s.s. *Soyuz vodnikov* ['Union of Watermen'— translator] had been detained in Gibraltar Bay. All through the succeeding months the attacks on Soviet vessels became more frequent, and sometimes ended in tragedy: on 14 December 1936 the Soviet steamship *Komsomol* was sunk near Gibraltar, and on 31 August and 1 September 1937 two more Soviet ships were lost, the *Timiryazev* and the *Blagoev*. The Soviet government protested repeatedly against this Fascist piracy, but owing to condonation on the part of Britain, France and the u.s.a. these protests had no practical result for a long time.

But the Fascist powers, encouraged by the inactivity of the 'appeasers', let themselves go more and more until in the end they were systematically hunting down the vessels of other powers as well (including those of Britain and France), if they were bound for Spanish Republican ports. Sometimes the attacks were made by warships under Franco's flag, sometimes by submarines and aircraft 'of unknown nationality'.

By the spring of 1937 the situation had become so acute that the representatives of the three Scandinavian countries—Sweden, Norway and Denmark—laid a complaint on 30 April before the Committee, in which they asked for emergency measures to be taken for the defence of shipping in Spanish waters. The u.s.s.r. fully supported the Scandinavians. Britain and France took up an ambiguous position; in words they expressed sympathy with the complaint, but in deeds displayed complete indifference. As a result the piratical actions of the Fascist powers assumed such monstrous forms and proportions in the summer of 1937 that not only democratic circles but the mighty shipping companies of Britain and France also raised loud cries of protest. This had a rapid and salutary effect.

On 10 September 1937 a conference met in Nyons (Switzerland), summoned on the initiative of Britain and France and involving nine powers (Britain, France, the u.s.s.r., Turkey, Greece, Yugoslavia, Rumania, Bulgaria and Egypt); at it the u.s.s.r., represented by the People's Commissar for Foreign Affairs, M. M. Litvinov, sharply posed the question of taking really serious measures against Fascist piracy. Since the interests of influential capitalist groups were involved here, the British and French representatives at Nyons took up an entirely different position from those in the Committee for 'Non-intervention'. The result of four days' work in the Conference was the signing, on 14 September 1937, of the Nyons Agreement, under which the naval forces of Britain and France took on the duty of patrolling the Mediterranean Sea. The other signatories to the Agreement undertook to patrol their own territorial waters. The patrol vessels were to open fire on any submarine attacking a non-Spanish ship. The effect of the Nyons Agreement surpassed all expectations. The wave of piracy in the Mediterranean at once subsided. During the winter of 1937–8 attacks on non-Spanish ships became a rare phenomenon . . .

However, I return now to the history of the British plan.

It was not until 16 October 1937 that discussion of the plan was reopened in London. This time it was the French government that took the initiative.

Having altered slightly the phrasing of the British plan, Corbin laid before the Committee a 5-point document, in which the only novelty was a proposal that there should be an immediate 'token withdrawal' of foreign combatants, for which the numbers fixed should take account of the proportion of forces on the two sides of the front. In his introductory speech Corbin stated that if these 5 points were not accepted without delay, the French government would consider that the policy of non-intervention had failed, and would reassume freedom of action for itself.

Plymouth fully supported the French representative and ended his speech in just the same way, with expressions of the British government's determination to reassume freedom of action if the present attempt to obtain unanimity should fail. It sounded almost like a threat to the Fascist powers. In the first minute I could not help thinking: 'Have Britain and France really learned a thing or two?' But then I remembered all that had gone on round that table during the past 13 months, and came to the conclusion: 'No, they are incorrigible.'

That conclusion was bitter, but correct.

The British and French attached great importance to the proposals put forward by Corbin. So great that at four meetings of the Sub-committee (on 19, 20, 22, 26 October 1937) the chair was taken not by Plymouth but by Eden, the British Foreign Secretary. London and Paris were terribly anxious to get the explosive Spanish question safely guided into 'constitutional channels', that is to strangle the Spanish Republic, but decently. Rome and Berlin could not fail to sympathise with this aim; the strengthening of the Spanish Republic, which had been so clearly achieved after the suppression of the Catalan *putsch* and the fall of the Caballero government, did not suit the Fascist powers at all. Ribbentrop and Grandi suddenly dripped sugar and honey. At the Sub-committee's meetings they were lavish with their compliments to Eden and Corbin, declared themselves ready to recognise the withdrawal of 'volunteers' as a task of prime importance, and poured their abuse and threats solely upon the U.S.S.R., which they made out to be the only obstacle standing in the way of universal agreement on the Spanish question.

Germany's and Italy's real intentions soon began to make themselves seen from behind this smoke-screen, however. They intended to use the French proposals as a spring-board, to obtain through them the immediate closure of the Franco-Spanish frontier and simultaneous recognition of belligerent rights for Franco. Six meetings of the Sub-committee between 19 October and 2 November were devoted to the French proposals, and in the course of their discussion the gradual *rapprochement* between Ribbentrop-and-Grandi and Plymouth-and-Corbin. By the end of it what in fact emerged was a *bloc* of the four Western powers, who were trying by every means at their disposal to put pressure on the u.s.s.r. and to force it to fall into step.

But the Soviet government stuck firmly to its own line. This meant the following two points: we demanded that the Spanish government have restored to it the right to buy arms where it wished, and we protested very definitely against granting Franco belligerent rights prior to the complete evacuation from Spain of foreign combatants.

Once they were convinced of the uselessness of trying to bring us round to their side at the Committee table, the four-power *bloc* began a rabid campaign against the u.s.s.r. in the press, on the radio, at public rallies and meetings, in Parliamentary debates.

The four Western powers were striving persistently to achieve complete isolation of the u.s.s.r., in order to free their own hands to assist Franco. This came out with particular clarity at the meeting of the Sub-committee on 22 October.

In its comments on the French proposals the Sovet government stated, among other things, that it could no longer bear the responsibility of continuing the policy of 'non-intervention', which it considered detrimental and unjust to the Spanish people and the Spanish government. Whereupon Eden, obviously with the sympathy of Ribbentrop, Grandi and Corbin, tried to interpret this statement as meaning that from then on the Soviet representative was remaining within the Committee only as an 'observer', that is without voting rights. However, I at once hastened to disillusion Eden, reminding him that 'the Soviet government is a member of the Committee for Non-Intervention', with all the consequences flowing therefrom. Eden and Corbin would not have minded having a debate on this point, but the Swedish representative Palmstierna came to my aid:

'Is not this discussion becoming rather academic? If we started on the practical points possibly it would help matters.'

Eden and Corbin had to abandon their idea, and in the meantime Palmstierna whispered in my ear: 'There are limits to every-thing . . .'

However, even after 22 October Ribbentrop and Grandi, following in Eden's footsteps, repeatedly tried to force the line that the decisions of the Committee had legal force even without the agreement of the U.S.S.R. The Soviet government in its fight to thwart these attempts showed not only firmness but its characteristic flexibility as well. I was instructed both to make every effort to have incorporated into the French version of the British plan amendments which would improve it (and we achieved significant results in this direction), and, on the other hand, to try to prevent our enemies from gaining material for further slanderous insinuations against the U.S.S.R. The final result was that at a plenary meeting of the Committee on 4 November it proved possible to accept a resolution whose main points were these:

1. The Committee accepts as a whole the British plan of 14 July 1937.

2. The Chairman of the Committee promptly to approach both sides in the Spanish conflict with this proposal: that they co-operate in the withdrawal of foreign nationals from Spain and agree to the Committee's sending two commissions there (one to Franco, one to the Spanish government) to make a record of the total number of foreigners taking direct part in the Spanish war, to prepare their evacuation and check on its effective execution.

3. The Chairman of the Committee to bring to the notice of the government of the Spanish Republic, also to that of General Franco, that each was to be accorded the status of a belligerent on the conditions laid down in the British plan of 14 July 1937.

4. Control over the Franco-Spanish frontier to be re-estab-lished a short time (about one week) prior to the actual evacu-ation of foreign combatants from Spain, when naval control also would be brought into effect.

5. All members of the Committee bind themselves to take the most energetic measures to halt the further flow of foreign nationals into Spain.

Acting on instructions from Moscow, I abstained when point 3 of this resolution was voted on (on granting of belligerent status), but supported the resolution as a whole. Ribbentrop and Grandi promptly took hold of this in order to whip up both inside and outside the Committee a new and vicious campaign against the U.S.S.R., alleging that our abstention on one point was equivalent to rejection of the whole resolution. And since their slanderous inventions were causing confusion in many heads in Europe, at the Sub-committee meeting of 16 November I announced on behalf of the Soviet government that the U.S.S.R. accepted the resolution of 4 November *in toto*.

In these actions the Soviet Union based itself on the fact that the considerably amended British control plan did not do any essential damage to Republican Spain, inasmuch as it left the Franco-Spanish frontier open until such time (if it came!) as the evacuation of foreign nationals from Spain should begin. As far as the question of belligerent status was concerned, the resolution of 4 November did not signify any final decision on this matter, it merely stated that such status could be accorded either side when (and if!) the Committee should agree that 'substantial progress' was being made in the evacuation of foreign combatants. In other words, the settlement of this question was put off into the future, and the Soviet Union retained the right to say its decisive word on this when it should deem it necessary.

In this way the U.S.S.R. by accepting the resolution in its entirety lost nothing essential and gained much tactically.

The Republican government and Franco were informed of this resolution through British diplomatic channels. Franco's answer arrived on 18 November and the Spanish government's on 30 November. In principle both were positive, although both had some reservations.

Franco, as usual, was insolent. He started off by declaring that he took this approach from the Committee to signify recognition of his 'government' by all the states represented on the Committee, and then demanded accordance of belligerent rights immediately upon withdrawal of 3,000 foreign nationals by each side in the Spanish conflict. I subjected this reply to sharp criticism, but in the end the Sub-committee accepted it as satisfactory and passed on to the elaboration of practical measures to implement the 4 November programme (formation of commissions to be sent to Spain, determination of methods to be followed and the limits of finance to be provided for the evacuation of foreign combatants, definition of belligerents' rights, etc.). This took up nine meetings of the Sub-committee and nearly 2 months' time (December 1937–January 1938).

Again fierce discussions raged. Again there was a stubborn struggle between the u.s.s.r. on the one hand and the Fascist powers on the other. Britain and France, in the last resort, almost always supported Germany and Italy.

The arguments on two questions became particularly acute.

The first of these concerned the financing of the evacuation. According to the preliminary estimates of the Sub-committee, the entire evacuation would cost about one and a half to two million pounds sterling. Quite an imposing sum!

Ribbentrop and Grandi insisted that the expense of evacuation must be divided evenly between Germany, Italy, Britain, France and the u.s.s.r. And Ribbentrop once again began to plead the poverty of Germany's resources in foreign currency and proposed that Germany's share should be paid in devalued marks. Grandi this time followed in his footsteps and declared that Italy would pay in her no less devalued lire. The most that the representatives of the Fascist powers would agree to was to cover their financial obligations 'in kind'.

Here was a paradox: the overwhelming majority of the foreign nationals in Spain were the Italians and Germans fighting on Franco's side, but the expense of their withdrawal was to be borne mainly by Britain, France and the u.s.s.r. Of course the Soviet government categorically refused to pay the expenses of Fascist intervention in Spain, and proposed that the expenses of the evacuation should be divided among the five Great Powers proportionally to the numbers of their citizens among the foreign combatants. This was just and rational. But Britain and France again took up a vague and ambiguous attitude, and the problem of financing the evacuation remained hanging in the air without any definite settlement.

The other question, which evoked even greater arguments in the Sub-committee, concerned the actual interpretation of the concept of 'substantial progress' in the evacuation of foreign combatants. After all, this was the factor on which recognition of belligerent rights for both Franco and the Spanish government was to be made dependent.

Foreseeing big differences in opinion, Plymouth made an attempt to sound out the ground for an agreement by 'private talks' with members of the Sub-committee. But he was definitely unlucky. He had to face the official meeting of the Sub-committee without having reached any sort of preliminary understanding at all.

The meeting on this question took place on 11 January 1938. The Soviet side took up a very firm stand here.

' "Substantial withdrawal" must be really substantial,' I said, 'that is, after it is effected the Spanish conflict must become a purely Spanish conflict and not a foreign war of aggression against the legitimate Spanish government.'

I went on to name actual figures. The Soviet government considered it possible to accept as a basis for interpretation of the term 'real progress' the evacuation from Spain of 80–85 per cent of the total number of foreign combatants.

The representatives of the Fascist powers did not dare to raise objections to this openly at this stage, and preferred to drag things out. First they recommended Plymouth to continue with his 'private talks' with individual members of the Sub-committee right up to a point at which some agreement might appear possible (which was obviously an impossibility). But Plymouth refused to do this, and Corbin supported him. Then the representatives of the Fascist powers proposed that the Sub-committee should discuss in order all the points of the programme of work for the Committee on the British plan, as prepared by Hemming. This caused me to raise determined objection.

'(I still believe) it would be very dangerous to tread the road suggested by the Italian and German Representatives. This document consists of 134 paragraphs, and that concerning substantial withdrawal is No. 133. Therefore, if we start our discussions . . . from the first paragraph onwards, I am afraid we shall come to paragraph 133 perhaps only in a few months' time.'

Our stand had a definite effect on Plymouth, Corbin and other representatives of the 'democratic' powers. They began to lean towards the opinion that 'substantial progress' in evacuation meant about 75 per cent of all foreign combatants being withdrawn. This was not too far from the figure we had named. But, as always, the representatives of Britain and France were unable to muster up sufficient firmness, and on meeting stubborn opposition from Ribbentrop and Grandi they began to retreat.

In the end the question of 'substantial progress' also was left hanging in the air.

On 3 February 1938 the Sub-committee held the last of a whole series of meetings devoted to working out the practical measures to put into effect the resolution of 4 November 1937. In spite of the fact that some questions remained unresolved, the British control plan had now taken shape to such an extent that it was possible to go on to at least the first stages of its realisation.

But here there happened something which at first glance seems incomprehensible. The entire work of the Committee, Sub-committee and all their numerous commissions stopped dead, as if at the wave of a magic wand, and this whole complex organism, full of inner contradictions, was for several months plunged into a state of prolonged suspended animation.

What was the matter?

The answer is to be sought in the events then taking place, not only in the Iberian peninsula, but also in the rest of Europe.

13

The wreck of hopes

IN spite of the loss of the Basque Country and the Asturias, the second half of 1937 was a period of consolidation and building-up of the forces of the Spanish Republic. This half-year was perhaps the highest point reached in its development, the time of the greatest hopes of final victory over the rebels and foreign interventionists.

There were several reasons for this. But the most important one was that just at this time signs could be clearly detected of a gradual healing of the split in the ranks of the Spanish proletariat (a phenomenon which had been the curse of the latter for decades). These signs related to both the Socialist and the Anarchist wing of the labour movement.

I shall take the former first. The Communist Party of Spain had long been devoting great and repeated efforts to the object of establishing friendly co-operation with the Socialist Party, but this had not found a sympathetic response from the other side. However, the bitter experience of war had compelled many Socialists to reconsider their attitude to the Communists, and had created a more favourable atmosphere for unity of action by the two parties. With this in mind, Dolores Ibárruri delivered a major report to a plenary meeting of the Central Committee of the Spanish Communist Party, in which the question of organisa-tional union with the Socialists was posed in all its great import. The new, unified Party of Spain's working class must be guided by the teaching of Marxism-Leninism's classical thinkers, and based on the principles of democratic centralism and iron discipline. Dolores Ibárruri formulated the aim of such a Party as follows:

'We are fighting for a Parliamentary and democratic Republic of a new type, within which all the peoples of Spain will enjoy wide freedom and the right to dispose of their own fate. In defence of this Republic we are ready to give all, to the last drop of our blood. But as Communists we do not abandon our desire to achieve the victory of Socialism in due time, and that not in Spain alone, but throughout the world.'

The meeting unanimously supported the speaker, and decided to continue the talks which had earlier been begun between the centres of the two Parties, Socialist and Communist. The right-wing Socialists, of course, did everything possible to sabotage the *rapprochement* with the Communists which seemed to be taking shape. The same was done by Largo Caballero, under cover of 'ultra-left' phrases. But the pressure from the mass of the workers in favour of joining forces was too great, and the majority of the Socialist Party followed Negrín, Alvarez del Vayo, Ramon Gonzales Peña, Ramon Lamoneda and other supporters of close co-operation with the Communists. The final result was the publication, on 17 August 1937, of the 'Programme of United Action of the Socialist and Communist Parties', the basic provisions of which were: improvement of the battle-worthiness of the People's Army and of the functioning of war industries; economic planning; establishment of a close alliance between workers and peasants; accordance of national rights to the peoples of Catalonia, Galicia and the Basque Country; achievement of unity within the trade-union and youth movements. This programme became the basis of the work of both the parties, and was widely applied in practice.

Real changes for the better were taking place within the Anarchist wing of the labour movement too. The lessons of war and revolution (especially the lessons of the Catalan *putsch*) resulted in something quite unheard-of in the history of Spanish anarchism: in July 1937 the famous Iberian Federation of Anarchists (known as the FAI), which had come into being ten

years previously and had existed all that time as a closed, under-
ground organisation with a few thousand members, decided to
become legal, and to turn itself into something which distinctly
resembled a political party of anarchists. The plenary meeting of
the Federation which took place at this time declared that 'the
FAI will not be able to fulfil its mission completely if the war is
lost', and therefore allowed anarchists to hold public office, and
recognised it as desirable that entry to the FAI should be open to
'every manual or intellectual worker who accepted the general
line and was willing to co-operate in realising it'.[1]

In view of the part played by the anarchists in Spain, these
decisions of the FAI also helped to make the political horizon
lighter. One result was the creation, on 1 August 1937, of a
National Committee of Liaison between the Socialist General
Union of Workers and the Anarcho-syndicalist National Confederation of Labour, complemented by analogous Liaison
Committees locally. Joint work and joint struggle by the two
trade-union centres (Socialist and Anarcho-syndicalist) drew
them closer together month by month, and in March of the
following year a Pact of Unity was signed.

Many other events of exceptional importance in the internal
life of Spain also belong to the second half of 1937. As has
already been mentioned above, this was the time when the
Republic began to reap the first-fruits from the immense efforts
previously put into the creation of the People's Army. The
period of the national militia was over. The foundations of a
united command had been laid. The International Brigades
became regular units of the Spanish army. The damaging
attempts made by Defence Minister Prieto to abolish the institution of military commissars came to nothing. A General Staff,
under Colonel Rojo, began to function. The formation of
reserves, the absence of which had made the successful development of actions in the field so difficult, now proceeded with
comparative speed.

The work of war industry also began to run more smoothly.

1. F. Jellinek, *The Civil War in Spain*, London, 1938, p. 571.

The Communist Party directed many of its best representatives into this work, and they fully justified the hopes placed in them. In spite of all the difficulties and obstacles, Spanish aircraft factories were started up and began to produce two or three aeroplanes a day. Many factories and plants previously non-military in character had by now successfully switched to war production. The flow of supplies or arms and ammunition to the army from home sources was noticeably improved.

Parallel with all this, for reasons dealt with above, the noose of 'non-intervention' slackened a little in this period. Of particular significance for the Republic and its army was the opening of the French frontier as from July 1937, and the practical cessation as from September, after the Nyons Conference, of Fascist piracy at sea.

However, against this generally favourable background one black spot stood out, the Aragon front. There the influence of the Catalan anarchists was still strongly felt, and this meant, in practice, that there was no real front ready to do battle on the Aragon sector. True, after the Catalan *putsch* the Aragon front was subjected to some reorganisation, something useful was undoubtedly achieved, but the old traditions none the less made themselves felt: discipline among the troops was distinctly lacking, the political work left much to be desired and the military leadership remained clearly inadequate.

Franco knew, of course, of this Achilles' heel of the Republic, and after his victory in the north began to prepare his 'final blow' here. The rebels' main forces were concentrated in Teruel. But the Republicans discovered in good time what was being planned against them, and decided to upset the enemy's plans by forestalling him and striking first. They succeeded in secretly concentrating on this sector about 50,000 men and 150 batteries of artillery. On 17 December the storm of Teruel was begun, and on the 22nd, in the midst of a terrible blizzard of snow (Teruel lies in the mountains), Republican units burst into the town, and after a short battle cleared it completely of rebel forces.

M

The battle of Teruel was a demonstration that the People's Army had learnt to attack as well as to defend itself. This had an immense effect in raising morale throughout the Republican camp.

In Franco's territory, on the other hand, the period under consideration saw revolts and uprisings occurring with ever-increasing frequency. In the first half of August 1937 there were major disturbances among the rebel troops on the southern front. In the middle of the same month there was a revolt of the Spanish garrison in Larache (Morocco), which was put down with the aid of the German air force. On 20 August the garrison of Saragossa rose in revolt, and German and Italian units had to be used to suppress them. On 10 October an army mutiny flared up in Jaca, and once again Franco brought in battalions of Italians and Moroccans against soldiers of Spanish nationality. Two hundred men were shot.

The number of such examples could easily be multiplied. As the Republic grew stronger, the more clearly did the symptoms of disintegration from within make themselves apparent on Franco's side.

On the eve of a new year, as 1938 approached, the Spanish Republic could look back with satisfaction and pride on the road she had travelled. Eighteen months ago she had begun a hard fight almost empty-handed. She had had neither army nor arms. Against her were openly ranged not only the Spanish rebels, but two extremely strong Fascist powers—Germany and Italy. Britain, France and the u.s.a. secretly thrust spokes into the wheel against her, inventing the farce of 'non-intervention'. The life of the Republic seemed to be hanging by a thread. But the heroism and revolutionary creative abilities of the masses had worked what might have seemed a miracle.

By the end of 1937 the Spanish Republic had been transformed into a real force, politically and militarily. Great hopes lent wings to her defenders. And these hopes were not high-minded fantasies. They had their basis in entirely real fact, so far as Spain itself was concerned.

But, unfortunately, the fate of Spain at that time was to be weighed in an alien balance; it depended, to the most marked degree, upon the struggle of other, imperialist powers. In the international arena the last acts prefacing the second world war were unfolding with dizzy speed. The menacing current of events was sucking all humanity into the abyss; and this found its fatal reflection in the course and outcome of the Spanish war.

The Fascist beast, personified first and foremost by Germany, had already unsheathed its claws, preparing for the spring that would lay all Europe prostrate beneath it. Yet the so-called 'democratic' powers, first of all Britain and France, with the sympathetic support of ruling circles in the u.s.a., still continued to coquette with the beast, hoping to turn the edge of aggression away to the East, against the Soviet Union.

On 19 November 1937 Lord Halifax, Lord President of the Council and Leader of the House of Lords, visited Hitler and 'had a talk with him on general political questions'. Hitler demanded, in excessively brazen tones, colonies for Germany and 'freedom of action in Europe'. Halifax assured him that if Germany came back into the League of Nations then there would be no especial obstacle to the satisfaction of her demands.

The British champion of 'appeasement' promptly enlarged on this:

'All the remaining questions [that is, besides that of the League of Nations—i.m.] could be characterised as relating to changes in the European order, changes that sooner or later would probably take place. To these questions belonged Danzig, Austria and Czechoslovakia. England was only interested that any alterations should be effected by peaceful evolution . . . The colonial question was undoubtedly difficult. The British Prime Minister was of the opinion that it could be settled only by way of a new start and as part of a general settlement.'[1]

These explanations by Halifax could have, and indeed had,

1. *Documents and Materials relating to the eve of the Second World War.* Pub. Ministry of Foreign Affairs of u.s.s.r., 1946, vol. 1, pp. 34–5.

only one meaning: Hitler's hands were to be left free in the East. The hypocritical-diplomatic declaration on the desirablity of making changes 'through peaceful evolution' did not alter the substance of the case. It was intended not for Hitler, but to fool simpletons in Britain and elsewhere. British imperialism, then, through the mouth of one of its most responsible representatives, gave its blessing to German Fascism to mount a general attack to the East, giving it to understand that in return for such a service one might even go so far as to return some of the colonies which had belonged to Germany before the first world war.

The attitude of the Chamberlain government raised the morale of all the Fascist forces in Europe. And this had its immediate repercussions on the international scene.

Mussolini now cast aside the fig-leaves from Italian intervention in Spain, and began to send more and still more divisions over. Besides which, he displayed a quite indecent insistence upon the conclusion of a Pact of Friendship and Political Co-operation between Britain and Italy.[1] The Foreign Secretary in Chamberlain's government, Eden, also a Conservative and an opponent of the Spanish Republic, but a more farsighted man than his chief, considered that Italy should 'buy' such a pact by stopping or at least reducing her aid to General Franco. This did not suit Mussolini. He himself and his press hurled thunder and lightning at Eden. In the end their aim was realised: on 20 February 1938 Eden was forced to resign, and his place was taken by . . . Lord Halifax. After this the Anglo-Italian talks at once advanced more rapidly, and on 16 April the Agreement which Mussolini so much desired was signed by Britain and Italy.

Did it touch upon the Spanish question? Yes, it did, but in such a form that Mussolini can only have applauded his British partner. The Agreement stated that Italy promised to withdraw her forces from the Pyrenean peninsula 'at the time and on the conditions fixed by the Committee for Non-Intervention, and that Britain shall ratify the Treaty concluded when the same

1. The talks about this had begun immediately Chamberlain came to power.

Committee shall declare the Spanish question "solved" '. This meant an undoubted victory for Mussolini.

Hitler was acting even more decisively. On 12 March 1938 he seized Austria and held his sword poised over Czechoslovakia (clearly he had heard and understood the words of his visitor Lord Halifax). As if in grim jest, the seizure of Austria took place on the very same day on which Chamberlain was holding a formal lunch in honour of Ribbentrop, who had just been appointed German Minister for Foreign Affairs.

Neither Britain, nor France, nor the u.s.a. found it necessary to come out against this new act of aggression on the part of Nazi Germany. Only the u.s.s.r. registered a firm protest. On 17 March 1938 the then People's Commissar for Foreign Affairs, M. M. Litvinov, held a press conference in Moscow in the course of which he invited the other powers to 'start prompt discussions inside and outside the League of Nations on the practical measures dictated by the circumstances'. Litvinov stressed particularly that after Austria it would be Czechoslovakia on whom the blow would fall next. But this warning too went unheeded.

I later handed the text of Litvinov's speech in to the Foreign Office, as instructed by Moscow, with an accompanying note underlining the fact that the enclosed speech represented the official view of the Soviet government. And what was the result? On 24 March the Chamberlain government replied that it considered premature the u.s.s.r.'s proposal that a conference be summoned.

France and the u.s.a. also remained deaf to the Soviet call.

Such behaviour by the 'democratic' powers encouraged Hitler even more to further acts of violence. From May 1938 onwards the so-called 'Czechoslovak crisis' was under way, accompanied by a threatening concentration of German troops on the borders of Czechoslovakia and a furious campaign in the Nazi press on the alleged 'persecution of the Sudeten Germans'. The warnings issued by the u.s.s.r. in March were proving justified! But the governments of Britain and France still, as before, took no effective measures to save this new victim of Fascism. French ruling circles were clearly anxious to evade fulfilment of their obligations as allies, under the Pact of Mutual Assistance France had signed with Czechoslovakia. As for the British cabinet, it played an even more indecent game.

At the end of August a 'mediator' between Prague and Berlin left Britain for Czechoslovakia—Lord Runciman, who in this capacity acted as an out-and-out 'appeaser', and by his proposals can only have made Hitler's undertaking easier for him.

The semi-official English press behaved no better. On 7 September 1938 there appeared in *The Times* the famous leading article proposing that the 'Czechoslovak crisis' be solved by handing the Sudetenland over to Germany.

In the last resort it all led up to the Munich deal, which wrote a page of ineradicable shame and stupidity into the history of British and French diplomacy.

In those difficult days only the Soviet Union did all in its power to make a real fight against Fascist aggression. On 2 September M. M. Litvinov made the French government aware that the U.S.S.R. was ready to fulfil its obligations under the Pact of Mutual Assistance with Czechoslovakia, and proposed that representatives of the Czechoslovak, French and Soviet General Staffs should be brought together to confer forthwith. Receiving no answer from Paris, he repeated this proposal publicly at a meeting of the League of Nations on 21 September. France again failed to respond.

The British proved more flexible. I remember that immediately following Litvinov's speech in the League of Nations an Anglo-Soviet conference took place in Geneva, on the initiative of the British. It was attended by Butler and Delaware on the British side, and Litvinov and myself on the Soviet side. Maxim Maximovich expended much energy in arguing the urgent need for joint action against the Fascist bandits. Butler and Delaware appeared to agree with us, declared that they would get in touch with London at once, after which we would meet again . . . Alas! the second meeting never took place. Butler and Delaware 'forgot' about it. And what else could they do? At this very time the preparatory work for the Munich deal was in full swing . . . And on the morning of 30 September Chamberlain, back from Munich, was at the London aerodrome waving the piece of paper he and Hitler had signed which was to ensure 'peace in our time' for mankind.[1]

1. The Anglo-German Declaration signed in Munich on 30 September 1938, on Chamberlain's initiative, in which it was said that the Four-power Agreement signed the previous day (by Germany, Italy, Britain and France) on the fate of Czechoslovakia, likewise the Anglo-German naval agreement of 1935, 'symbolised the will of the two peoples never to go to war with one another again'. This declaration in effect offered Hitler complete freedom of action so far as other nations were concerned, and enabled Chamberlain to mislead the masses of the British people, who were gravely concerned by the policy of 'appeasement' of the aggressors.

The Nemesis of history exacted a cruel repayment from Britain and France for the treachery of Munich. Chamberlain and Daladier fell into their own trap. In unleashing the second world war Germany struck her first blows not against the u.s.s.r., but against France, Britain and Poland (then closely associated with them).

14

Agony and death of the Committee
for 'Non-intervention'

THE conflagration that blazed in the Iberian peninsula was becoming a progressively more and more irritating annoyance to Chamberlain's government. From the time when he set course firmly for a deal with the Fascist powers and made it his aim to turn the point of Hitler's aggression to the East, the British Premier's main concern was to douse as quickly as possible the flames of this conflagration. The best thing from his point of view would be to get rid of the Spanish war by means of a compromise of some sort (let it be rotten in substance, so long as it be decent in form). And if a compromise was impossible, then let Franco win as soon as possible ...

With such attitudes prevalent in British ruling circles (and French ones too), the entire British plan, the object of which was to create some kind of equilibrium between the two warring sides in Spain, became a dangerous anachronism for the 'appeasers', and further discussion of it in the Committee, which always provoked sharp polemics both at the Committee table and in the world press, no longer made sense for them. That is why Plymouth, as early as 3 February 1938, asked the members of the Sub-committee not to fix the date of their next meeting but to leave it to the discretion of the Chairman, who would proceed 'according to the prevailing circumstances'. Plymouth explained this as being due to his needing time for private talks with separate members of the Committee to settle certain disputed questions.

The pause lasted nearly 2 months. The Sub-committee only met again on 31 March. The disputed questions, however, still remained unsettled.

Plymouth put forward a new proposal for the solution of the most important of the points on which there was disagreement—the interpretation of 'substantial progress' in the withdrawal from Spain of foreign nationals. He proposed that 'substantial progress' should be considered as having been made if the side having the lesser number of foreign combatants should have evacuated 12–15,000 of these, and the opposing side—a number representing the same proportion for them as the 12–15,000 did for their opponents.

There was a brief and not very lively debate, as a result of which the majority of the Committee's members went on record in favour of the starting figure being made somewhat lower—10,000 men to be withdrawn. Plymouth, of course, did not object. I behaved with great caution at this meeting, and took practically no part in the discussion. My reasoning ran like this:

'The strength of the International Brigades at present is not more than 12–13,000. So if the starting figure is accepted as 10,000 men, that will be 78–80 per cent of the strength of the Brigades. And Franco, correspondingly, will lose three-quarters of his foreign troops. Well, that would not be too bad at all! . . .'

It looked as though the possibility of agreement on the most difficult point of the British plan was in sight. It only remained for the Sub-committee to do all it could to speed up its work. But this did not chime in with the true intentions of the Chamberlain and Daladier governments. The last thing likely to appeal to them would have been any easing of the struggle for Republican Spain. They passionately wanted to remove entirely from the agenda, one way or another, the wretched 'Spanish question', which was spoiling their hand in their big play with Hitler and Mussolini. The tenacity of life of the Spanish Republic, which continued, come what might, to put up a heroic resistance to the Fascists, reduced the English and French leaders to despair; and they did what they could to get the Republic into its grave as soon as possible. So it is not so surprising that when the discussion was over at the meeting of 31 March, Corbin delicately indicated, with the obvious support of the majority, that on this occasion also the choice of a date for the next meeting would be best left to Plymouth. The result was that everything once again froze into immobility for almost 2 months. A fresh meeting of the Sub-committee, to discuss the British plan, did not take place until 26 May.

By this time the situation in Europe generally and in Spain in particular had become very grim. On 12 March 1938 Hitler seized Austria and had his sword poised over Czechoslovakia. On 16 April Chamberlain signed the Treaty of Friendship and Co-operation with Mussolini. Heartened by its easy successes, Fascism reared its repulsive head everywhere and its foul breath poisoned the political atmosphere of Europe. Such a course of events strengthened the belief in Franco's camp that final victory was near, all the more so since Germany and Italy had now begun quite openly sending whole armies and immense quantities of arms to Spain. From the beginning of 1938 the Fascist aggressors on Spanish soil had gone over to the attack on a broad scale, and by 21 February the Republicans had lost Teruel, which they had taken so brilliantly 2 months previously.

And 2 weeks after Teruel had been given up, the Spanish democrats suffered a further reverse. The Fascists, having assembled a striking force of 10 divisions, with thousands of guns, hundreds of tanks, and air cover of 800 planes, launched a heavy attack on the Aragon front. The main mass of the attacking troops consisted of Italians (50,000), Moroccans (30,000) and Germans (10,000). The Republican forces forming the defence here were considerably inferior both in numbers and in armaments. Suffice it to say that against the 800 enemy planes they could only muster 60.

For 10 days the Fascists advanced almost without meeting any opposition. Only by the end of March did Colonel Modesto, and other Republican officers hastily transferred from other fronts, succeed in somewhat slowing down the enemy advance. To halt it completely was already impossible. On 15 April 1938 the Fascists broke through to the Mediterranean coast between Tortosa and

Valencia. The Spanish Republic was now split into two parts: to the north there was Catalonia, and to the south and south-west the central sector, including Madrid, Valencia, Cartagena and a number of other most important points. The corridor held by the Fascists was not wide, but it complicated the Republic's position considerably for all that.

The Aragon break-through had great political and military repercussions. All the reactionary forces of Europe, all the supporters of 'non-intervention', at once felt their spirits rise. They thought that now it really was true that the end of the Spanish Republic was a matter of a few days' time, or at most a few weeks'. I remember that it was just at this time that I had to talk to Plymouth, who was continuing his everlasting 'individual consultations'. Having completed the business part of the conversation, he said confidentially: 'I hope I shall not have to bother you about Spanish affairs for much longer . . . Events in Spain are moving to their close, the end is near . . .'

'Do you think so?' I said doubtfully.

'But of course,' replied Plymouth. 'The Republic has suffered such a heavy blow that it will never recover.'

And he added with relief: 'Soon I shall be able to breathe again . . . I assure you, never in my life have I had such a troublesome business on my hands as the Committee for Non-intervention . . . But it's finished now!'

I smiled and reminded him: 'Mr. Grandi, the Italian Ambassador, was foretelling the end of the Spanish Republic in a few days' time back in November 1936. It is April 1938 now, and the Spanish Republic is still alive and fighting.'

My reminder clearly spoilt Plymouth's good mood. He passed his hand over his head, as if brushing away unpleasant thoughts, and remarked more vaguely: 'The future will show . . .'

Corbin, with whom I talked in the same period at a reception, expressed himself in the same vein. He was merely more frank:

'I understand very well,' said the French Ambassador, 'that the death of the Spanish Republic augurs no good for France . . . on the long-term view, that is . . . but just now . . . Now we are

in such difficulties, such confusion, we are so full of internal
contradictions, that we are ready to welcome any end to the
"Spanish question" without stopping to think of the future. . . .
Maybe we shall get a breathing-space then, for a little while at
least, and shall be able to think of some way of saving Europe.'

History did not grant such a breathing-space to either Europe
or France: just six months after Franco's victory the guns of the
second world war spoke out. . . .

Corbin's delusions, like Plymouth's prophecies, undoubtedly
reflected the view-points of their governments.

It was literally the day after the Fascists broke through to the
Mediterranean that Chamberlain signed the Treaty of Friendship
and Co-operation, which has already been mentioned, with Italy.
The French government in its turn, after previously allowing the
Republicans to import arms across French territory, now began
to slow the process down by various means, and in June closed
the Franco-Spanish frontier completely. At the same time the
campaign of piracy by submarines and aircraft of 'unknown
nationality' began once more in Spanish waters. Yes, all the
'appeasers' of Europe and America now thought that the abyss
was gaping for the Spanish Republic, and each of them hastened
to get in some dirty trick before it was too late, so as to be able
to say later: 'I helped to kick them over the edge.'

The 'appeasers', however, had yet one more bitter disappointment in store for them. The Aragon break-through had had
consequences within Spain that were not all negative. In face of
this mortal danger all that was revolutionary, democratic and
progressive in the country rose up in one heroic wave, and
redoubled the efforts put into the struggle against the Fascist
aggressors. The people of the Republic—men, women and even
the children—inspired above all by the example set by the
Communists, performed wonders of bravery, endurance and self-
lessness. Pulling in their belts and gritting their teeth, the
supporters of the Republic fought a merciless fight with the foe,
each wherever he was and however he could. This mighty concentration of thought and will on one great idea, on one over-

riding aim, produced a gigantic revolutionary energy. The result was that in spite of the ever-increasing superiority of forces on the Fascist side, the Spanish Republic held out for another year.

The sequence of events was as follows:

On 4 April 1938, when the full extent of the failure of the Aragon front had just become clear, a governmental crisis blew up. The main bearer of responsibility for the disaster in Aragon was without a doubt the Minister of Defence, Indalecio Prieto. This right-wing Socialist, who had long since lost all faith in both the people and the possibility of Republican victory, had by the spring of 1938 become a complete defeatist. All his thoughts were concentrated on concluding 'peace at any price' with Franco.

Prieto had an extremely negative attitude to the institution of military commissars. Prieto took no effective measures against the scandalous proceedings of the anarchists on the Aragon front. And when at last the Fascist break-through to the Mediterranean showed up so unmistakably all the wrongness of his policies, he became simply impossible to retain as a member of the government.

On 5 April Negrín formed a new government, which personified the union of all the democratic forces in the Republic which were prepared to fight to a finish. The government included Socialists, Communists, Left Republicans, Catalan and Basque nationalists, also (and this was especially important!) representatives of both the trade union centres—the Socialist Universal Union of Workers and the Anarcho-syndicalist National Confederation of Labour. The most important post in the cabinet at that time, that of Defence Minister, was taken over by the Premier, Negrín. The second Negrín government declared itself a War Cabinet and on 30 April 1938 issued a declaration of war aims. This Declaration consisted of 13 points, among which were these:

entire independence and entire territorial integrity of Spain;

a People's Republic, based on the principles of pure democracy;

a plebiscite when the war was over;

respect for regional privileges without detriment to the territorial integrity and unity of Spain;

a far-reaching agrarian reform with the aim of eliminating the
old, aristocratic, semi-feudal property;

progressive social legislation for the workers; a higher level of
cultural, physical and moral well-being for the nation;

renunciation of war as an instrument of national policy.

Particularly characteristic for this government was Point 7 of
its programme, which dealt with the question of property. This
point guaranteed on the one hand the inviolability of 'property
acquired in a lawful and legal manner', and promised on the other
'to work against the accumulation of wealth leading to the
exploitation of citizens and the subordination of the collective,
thus depriving the government's measures of control over
economic and social life of their due effect'. Point 7, like this
programme as a whole, undoubtedly bore the imprint of compromise reached between the various parties participating in the
second Negrín government. None the less, though, considering
this document as a whole one cannot but recognise it as a considerable step forward. Not for nothing did Dolores Ibárruri, at
a plenary meeting of the Central Committee of the Communist
Party in May 1938, call the new government's programme 'most
concrete, most broad and historically correct'.

The constitution of the second Negrín government was
followed by important reforms, which activated both front and
rear. Measures were taken to strengthen unity of command. The
system of military commissars was restored in its full extent. A
Decree was published (on 24 April) mobilising various sections
of the population. The administration of factories producing
arms and ammunition was improved. Efforts to get war materials
from abroad were redoubled. The training of reinforcements and
reserves was speeded up, and went on apace in the streets of towns
and villages. All Republican Spain became one great military
camp. The whole people was up in arms against defeatists and
spreaders of despondency.

These events inside Spain gave a strong impetus to a new wave of sympathy for the defenders of her freedoms, among democratic groupings in Europe and other continents. Again there were meetings, demonstrations, questions in Parliament. Again the shipowners of Britain, France and Scandinavia raised a great noise about the piratical attacks which had once more become frequent on ships in Spanish waters. Again the press and radio were full of articles and reports on the war in Spain, and many of these expressed obvious sympathy for the Republican side.

In such a situation the British and French governments found themselves obliged to do something to lessen even a little the atmosphere of tension which was building up. In London and Paris they remembered about the Committee for 'Non-intervention'. A little camphor was injected into its stiffening members, and for a short time they began to function as if alive.

On 26 May 1938 Plymouth suddenly summoned together the Sub-committee, and after shedding the regulation number of crocodile tears over the prolonged pause in its activities, addressed to those present a no less hypocritical appeal to get that cumbrous vehicle the British plan moving once again, since 'the international situation is far from easy, and one of the problems making for that uneasiness and sense of insecurity is the position obtaining in regard to Spain'. The Sub-committee started to work with an energy such as had not been seen for a long time, and in the course of 7 meetings (on 26 and 31 May, and 2, 21, 24, 28 and 30 June) did in fact prepare an agreed text of the British plan.

I personally did not take part in this last burst of life in the Committee for 'Non-intervention'. In the middle of May 1938, when there was not the slightest sign of this death-bed paroxysm of activity, the People's Commissariat of Foreign Affairs had given me permission to go on leave to the u.s.s.r. And even after the paroxysm had become perfectly well defined, the Soviet government did not urge me to make haste to return to England: in Moscow they were not cherishing any illusions.

In this last period of feverish activity in the Committee, the u.s.s.r. was represented in it by Counsellor of the Embassy

S. B. Kagan. And one must give him his due—he showed himself in his best light there.

The main difficulties to be solved at this stage were three.

First, there needed to be a final definition of what, concretely, the term 'substantial progress' in the withdrawal of foreign nationals from Spain was to mean. The U.S.S.R., as has already been said, demanded that 'substantial progress' should mean the withdrawal of 80–85 per cent of the total number of foreign nationals. Plymouth in effect agreed with us, but went about it in a roundabout way. In the end the formula accepted was the one proposed by Plymouth, which if put into effect would mean the removal from Spain of at least 75 per cent of the Italians and Germans fighting on Franco's side. So the U.S.S.R. succeeded in gaining an important point here.

Secondly, it had to be established just when the Franco-Spanish frontier was to be closed to the transit of arms shipments. The resolution adopted by the Committee on 4 November 1937 provided for this being done approximately one week prior to the actual evacuation of foreign combatants. And their actual evacuation could only begin when the estimating commissions sent by the Committee into the Republican zone and to Franco should have completed their calculations, when all the foreign combatants should have been withdrawn from the front and gathered into special camps, and when a sufficient number of transports should have been concentrated in Spanish ports to ship them out. The same resolution provided for re-establishment of control on the Franco-Spanish frontier accompanied by simultaneous re-establishment of naval control (in the form either of patrols along the Spanish borders, as previously, or in the shape of control officers of the Committee installed in Spanish ports). The U.S.S.R. stood for the strictest observation of this condition. The representatives of the Fascist powers, on the other hand, used every possible means to achieve the re-establishment of control on the Franco-Spanish frontier as early as possible and to put off the re-establishment of naval control for as long as possible. Plymouth and Corbin sat on the fence between us and the Fascists, gradually leaning more and more in the direction of the German and Italian position. However, thanks to the firmness of the Soviet government our demands won the day on this question also.

Thirdly, it had finally to be decided how and by whom the evacuation of foreign combatants was going to be financed. I well recall to mind that the Fascist representatives wanted all the expenses of the evacuation (coming to something in the region of £1½–£2 million) to be divided equally between the five Great Powers—Britain, France, the U.S.S.R., Germany and Italy. The Soviet government, on the contrary, proposed that the expenses should be divided among the various states according to the respective numbers of their citizens being evacuated. Britain and France again wavered between us and the Fascists. But in the last resort the following compromise was reached: the expenses of maintaining the apparatus which the Committee must have in order to carry out the evacuation (estimating commissions, observing officers in Spanish ports, etc.) were to be borne in equal parts by the five Great Powers; the expenses of keeping the foreign combatants in special camps in Spain while they awaited evacuation were to be borne by the Republican government and Franco respectively; while the expenses of actual evacuation by sea or rail were to be paid by the governments of the countries from which the combatants came. So here also the U.S.S.R. had no cause for complaint.

And now, on 5 July 1938, the plenary meeting of the Committee was gathered together to adopt the plan worked out by the Sub-committee. This meeting had been heralded by a great fuss in the press and in political circles in Britain and France. To lend more weight to the meeting it was chaired not by Plymouth, but—again—by the British Foreign Secretary, this time Lord Halifax. He made an opening speech suitable to the occasion, in which he thanked all the members of the Committee for the spirit of co-operation they had shown, and expressed the hope that the present meeting 'may prove to be of good augury and omen for the carrying through in the international field of a very novel

N

and a very complicated piece of real international co-operation'.

Then, after a brief and unaccustomedly calm discussion, in the course of which some individual and very minor details were cleared up, the entire British plan in its last version was unanimously adopted by the Committee for 'Non-intervention'.

This was to be its last meeting. After this the Committee again fell into a state of suspended animation, and its unburied corpse stank for ten whole months more, poisoning the political atmosphere of Europe.

Meanwhile the war in Spain went on.

After the Aragon break-through the Fascist aggressors made their next object the widening of the narrow corridor which they had driven to cleave Spain into two parts. The next blow was aimed at Valencia. It was begun on 15 July, that is, ten days after the Committee for 'Non-intervention' had adopted the British control plan.

The aggressors advanced against the temporary capital of the Spanish Republic an army of 8,000 men, with 600 guns and 400 planes. The main body of troops, again, were Italians.

The Republicans succeeded in holding the Fascists in the mountain passes, and on 25 July an army 60,000 strong, under the command of Modesto, suddenly forced the river Ebro and inflicted a powerful blow on the flank of the Franco forces. Panic broke out in the enemy ranks, and they began a hasty retreat. In five days the Republicans advanced 45 kilometres and seized a vast quantity of enemy arms and supplies.

Franco's intention of widening the corridor across Republican Spain had been brought to naught. This corridor had become even a little narrower. Here was new, brilliant proof of the growing strength of the Republican army.

Unfortunately, however, the government had not sufficient reserves at its disposal to enable it to develop this initial success and utilise it to the full. The forward impetus of the Republican troops was fairly soon exhausted, and Modesto's army was obliged to pass over to the defensive, without having achieved complete break-up of the Fascist forces.

The enemy, of course, took advantage of this. Having received fresh reinforcements from abroad, he renewed the attack. The Republicans had to fall back. They retreated slowly, with heavy fighting, and inflicting grave losses on the enemy, but they retreated. By 15 November 1938 the government troops were back the other side of the Ebro once more.

Now the Fascist aggressors were able to set about preparing the 'final battle' for Catalonia. For this they massed 120,000 men, mainly Italians. The Italian general Gambara was in direct charge of the operation. Among the attacking forces there were also some Navarrese divisions, several Moroccan divisions, and the whole of the Spanish 'foreign legion'. Gambara had at his disposal 200 tanks, 500 guns (including 100 pieces of heavy artillery) and almost 1,000 aircraft (including the German 'Condor Legion').

On the Republican side the picture was very different. True, the numbers of men involved were about the same—around 120,000 —but for the whole of this army there were only 37,000 rifles! There were not more than one or two machine-guns per battalion. Not many army corps had more than 28 light guns. Of heavy artillery there was none at all. There was a dire shortage of anti-aircraft guns. And in the air there was one Republican plane against 10–20 Fascist aircraft.

The balance of forces was uneven to the point of catastrophe. Yet it could easily have been altered in the Republic's favour. During the preceding months the Republican government had managed, because of immense efforts, to buy in various countries 500–600 aircraft, 30 fast torpedo-boats and a large quantity of artillery and ammunition. At the beginning of the battle for Catalonia all this was just on the other side of the Franco-Spanish frontier. And however much the Republican government pleaded, France would not hand these goods over to their rightful owner, although the British control plan had not yet been brought into operation.

The Communist Party of France put a motion to the military commission of the Chamber of Deputies that the military property of the Spanish Republic be promptly transferred to Catalonia. If this had been done, the whole course of the battle for Catalonia, and perhaps the fate of Spain itself, might have been quite different. But the Daladier government was deliberately out to kill the Spanish Republic, and therefore refused completely to open the Franco-Spanish frontier.

I cannot describe in detail all the phases and stages of the battle for Catalonia which took place in December 1938 and January 1939. I shall say only that in spite of the greatest heroism, displayed not by the army alone but the local population also, the Fascists nevertheless moved forward, step by step. Masses of refugees appeared. Unending crowds of people flooded all the roads leading to the north, towards France. Old men, women and children toiled along on foot, rode on donkeys, in carts, in cars, in lorries. Through the cold nights of January they slept on the bare ground, afraid to light fires in case they attracted the attention of enemy aircraft.

The farther the interventionists penetrated, the larger grew the crowds of refugees. Some irresistible impulse drove people to leave their hearths and homes, to do anything rather than remain under the Fascist yoke. In the end the whole of this vast and troubled sea of half a million human beings swept up to the French frontier and began to beat insistently upon the gates of France.

And the fighting took its course. On 26 January Barcelona fell, and on 5 February, Jerona. All that remained in Republican hands was a tiny corner in the north-east of Catalonia, centred round the small town of Figueras. To this town the Republican government and the Cortes had been evacuated.

On 1 February 1939 the Cortes decided that the government must initiate peace talks with Franco (in practice, this meant with Germany and Italy) on the basis of the following three points:

1. Evacuation of all foreigners fighting on Franco's side.

2. Freedom for the Spanish people to choose whatever form of government it wished.

3. Guarantees that no reprisals would be undertaken against Republican supporters.

The government asked Britain and France to act as mediators, but they took their time to reply. Why should they hurry! Chamberlain and Daladier were viewing their handiwork with satisfaction, and did not want to do anything to hinder the 'natural course of events'.

Under these conditions nothing remained for the Republican army, and for the vast mass of refugees crowding together at the French border, but to seek safety in France.

As early as 22 January the Spanish Minister of Foreign Affairs, Alvarez del Vayo, had approached the French Foreign Minister Bonnet with a request that the Spanish refugees be admitted to French territory, but Bonnet refused categorically. This called forth profound indignation in democratic French circles, especially among the workers. The Daladier government had to make concessions; the frontier was opened just a crack, and small trickles of Spanish refugees began to filter through. Wounded soldiers of the Spanish army were also conveyed across the border to the French side. But on 28 January the French government again closed the frontier completely, and even returned all the wounded to Catalonia. The French population along the border was strictly forbidden to give any aid whatsoever to the Spaniards.

A few more days passed thus.

But on 3 February the Italian air force made a mass attack on Figueras. Over 1,000 people were killed or wounded.

Panic broke out among the refugees. They rushed the French frontier and broke through all the cordons. The Daladier government was forced to give retrospective sanction to what had already happened. It officially opened the frontier to refugees and to retreating units of the Republican army.

By 9 February all was over. The refugees and the remnants of the troops of the Spanish Republic were in France. What awaited them there?

For the refugees the Daladier government hastily arranged several huge concentration camps (at Saint-Cyprien, Prat de Molleau and in other places). The tens of thousands of famished, worn-out people locked up in these camps were left without water, without bread, without soap, on the bare sand-dunes. Epidemics started, the mortality was on a monstrous scale. But the Daladier cabinet was not perturbed.

The same fate was in store for the soldiers. A special camp was made for them at Argilles. This was where the best units of the Republican army went, those which had maintained discipline and fighting power even at the very end of the battle for Catalonia. In France they were made to give up their arms and, like the refugees, cast on the bare ground. There was nothing to eat or drink. They were treated worse than prisoners of war. The police authorities mocked, in all manner of ways, at the heroes of the Spanish revolution.

Thus the France of the 'two hundred families' greeted the people who for almost three years had waged a selfless struggle not only for their own freedom, but for the security of the French people as well. It is hard to imagine a greater degree of moral depravity and political blindness!

As for Britain, at this very time she was rendering active assistance to Franco in the seizure of the island of Minorca, which throughout the whole war had been a base for the Republic. The British cruiser *Devonshire* played a shameful part in this.

The 'appeasers' in London, Paris and Washington thought that now the end had really come for the Spanish Republic! But the end was not yet. Under the control of the legitimate government of the Republic there still remained the central-southern zone, comprising about one-quarter of the country's territory, with a coastline of 700 kilometres, and with such major cities as Madrid, Valencia and Alicante within it. Also in Republican hands was the main naval base of Cartagena, a considerable naval force, and a number of factories producing armaments. All this made continued resistance to the Fascists for a comparatively long period quite possible. At the same time the international situation at the beginning of 1939 was so inflamed that at any moment events might occur which would change the outlook in a way favourable to the Republic. So that even after the lost battle for Catalonia there was no need to lose heart. The fight must go on to the last. That was the position taken up by the Communist Party of Spain. Unfortunately, however, on this occasion its efforts were not crowned with success. There were two reasons for this.

The first reason lay in the fact that after the loss of Catalonia defeatist attitudes began to gain ground among the Socialists, Anarchists and Left Republicans. True, the Negrín government, which had been evacuated to France along with the remnants of the Catalan army, later returned to the central-southern zone, but the miasma of decomposition had penetrated even into its midst. The government, and its Premier Negrín in particular, clearly lacked fighting spirit, decision and the ability to take the long view. It took up a kind of half-hearted position, and so was incapable of making use of the possibilities of continued resistance which in fact existed.

The second reason was a matter of foreign policies. Speculating on the disaffection in the Republican camp, the London and Paris 'appeasers' finally cast aside the hypocritical mask of 'non-intervention' and came out openly against the Spanish Republic.

On 27 February 1939 Britain and France officially recognised Franco and broke off diplomatic relations with the Republican government. This was only the prelude. On 5–6 March a counter-revolutionary revolt broke out in Madrid, led by the right-wing Socialist Besteiro and the officer in command of the Republican central front, Colonel Casado. This revolt was organised by Chamberlain's agents, with friendly aid from those of Daladier. Negrín did not manage to put down the revolt (although the forces to do it were there), and as a result his cabinet had to seek refuge in France for the second time, this time not to return. The conspirators seized power. They opened the front to Franco and turned with bestial cruelty against units which remained loyal to the Republic, under the command of Communist officers. Then, when the black deed of treason was done, Casado and a hundred or so of his supporters set sail for England, on 1 April 1939, on board the British cruiser *Galatea*. It seemed good to Chamberlain to give this last small recognisance to those who had at his government's bidding thrust the knife into the back of the Republic.

Well, and what of the Committee for 'Non-intervention'? How did it behave in the course of these 9 months which put the finishing touches to the tragedy of the Spanish war?

I shall list the most important facts.

After 5 July 1938, practically speaking its only functioning parts were Lord Plymouth and the secretariat under Francis Hemming. This rump of the Committee made use of the mediating services of the British government in order to send the control plan adopted at the Committee's last meeting to the Republican government and to Franco, after which it settled down to wait.

On 26 July an answer was received from the Republican government. It was in the affirmative. With Franco it was otherwise.

When I returned to London from my leave, at the end of July, I tried several times to find out from Lord Plymouth what was happening in relation to the plan, on the far side of the front, but I could not get any satisfaction. The honourable Lord became more and more like the Delphic oracle, which as we know was famous for the ambiguity and vagueness of its answers. One thing was clear to me: things were not going well for the plan.

We now know in full detail, from the documents captured by the Soviet army in Germany, how both Franco and his German and Italian patrons treated that long-suffering document.

In a telegram dated 15 July 1939, the German Ambassador to Franco, Storer, informed Berlin that he had had a talk about the Committee's plan with Franco's Minister for Foreign Affairs, Jordan, and had urged him 'to find ways of strengthening Chamberlain's position by expressing agreement in principle to this plan'.[1]

What touching solicitude on the part of the Fascists for the well-being of the British Prime Minister!

1. *Documents of the German Ministry for Foreign Affairs*. Pub. Ministry for Foreign Affairs of u.s.s.r., 1946, series 3, pp. 52–4.

A day later, on 16 July, the German Ambassador to Rome, Mackensen, wrote in a report to Ribbentrop:

'The Italian government is of the opinion that for political reasons it would be very desirable to advise Franco to inform the London Committee forthwith that he accepts the London plan in principle. In the Note which he should send to the Committee he could declare that he is studying the plan carefully and will shortly be sending on his observations on each separate point of the plan. Later (and there is no need to hurry over it) Franco will send a second Note, containing detailed comments and appropriate counter-questions . . . The London plan offers great opportunities for objections and counter-questions'.[1]

In the end the method proposed by the Italian government was followed.

A long delaying action by the Fascist powers began. It was vitally necessary to them, since this was the precise period in which the attack on Catalonia was being prepared, and the German and Italian interventionists were hastily conveying new reinforcements and new consignments of arms to Franco.

It was only on 12 August that Franco at last found time to send the Committee his first Note, in which he assured them that his reply had been delayed 'owing entirely to the complicated nature of the plan'. On 20 August the second Note from Franco arrived, containing a number of questions on different points in the plan, also his own counter-proposals.

Plymouth was not in a hurry either. He took plenty of time to 'study' each of Franco's Notes, and then saw fit to despatch the Committee's Secretary Francis Hemming to Burgos and to Barcelona 'to get a clearer and more exact understanding' of the answers received from Franco and from the Republican government.

Thus, while in the autumn of 1938 the fighting on the Ebro was in progress and the Fascists were preparing their attack on Catalonia, an unhurried game of diplomatic pat-ball went on between Franco and Plymouth, which suited perfectly the

1. Ibid., p. 56.

interests of the aggressors. In this instance the British government once again played the part of a direct accomplice of German and Italian intervention in Spain.

A certain discordant note was introduced into this play between the open and the concealed patrons of General Franco, by a bold act on the part of the Spanish government.

On 23 September 1938, at a meeting of the Council of the League of Nations, Negrín announced that his cabinet had decided to act unilaterally, without waiting for the plan of the 'Non-intervention' Committee to come into operation, and were going to evacuate from the territory of the Republic all the International Brigades in their entirety (at that time they numbered about 10,000), and requested the League of Nations to send a commission to check on the execution of this decision.

This action of the Republican government put the Fascists and their 'appeasers' in a difficult position. The logic of things demanded that after 100 per cent evacuation of the foreign combatants on the Republican side there should follow the same on Franco's part. But what a hope! Prior to the battle for Catalonia Franco was demanding more and still more reinforcements from his German and Italian masters. And they did not refuse him. The Fascist powers did not react at all to the Republican government's decision on the International Brigades.

The position of the 'democratic' powers, Britain in particular, was more complicated. As I have already mentioned, the ratification of the Anglo-Italian Treaty of Friendship and Cooperation of 16 April 1938 had been made directly dependent upon the withdrawal from Spain of the Italian 'volunteers'. But Mussolini had not the slightest intention of doing this. What was to be done . . . ? Then the sages of the British Foreign Office found a way out: on 9 October 1938 Franco declared that he also was voluntarily, by unilateral decision, evacuating 10,000 foreign nationals who had been fighting on his side for more than 18 months (in fact these were all sick and wounded). Even after their departure, Franco still had about 150,000 German and Italian troops!

It was an obvious piece of chicanery, but Chamberlain preferred to close his eyes to this so evident deception. He pretended that Mussolini had really fulfilled his obligation to evacuate the Italian 'volunteers' from Spain, and on 16 September 1938 he ratified the Anglo-Italian Treaty. And two months later, at the very height of the battle for Catalonia, the British Premier together with Lord Halifax paid a 'visit of friendship' to Mussolini. It was equivalent to giving the Fascist dictator complete absolution from all his sins in Spain.

More than that, when Chamberlain returned to Britain and was to give an account in the House of Commons of his visit to Rome, he sent the text of his speech for Mussolini to see beforehand, a fact unheard-of in the political annals of Britain. Such was the pitch of intimacy reached between the leader of Italian Fascism and the Prime Minister of 'democratic' Great Britain! . . .

Now the London control plan was finally dead. Finally dead, also, was the Committee for 'Non-Intervention'. The Soviet government drew the only possible correct conclusion, and on 4 March 1939 the TASS agency published the following statement:

'In connection with the fact that the London Committee for "Non-Intervention" has long since ceased to function and has lost its reason for existing, the Council of People's Commissars of the U.S.S.R. decided on 1 March of this year to recall their representative from the Committee for "Non-Intervention".'

And on 20 April 1939 the Committee as a whole officially ceased to be.

In conclusion it only remains for me to quote one very expressive assessment of the whole saga of 'non-intervention', an assessment made by a former Minister for Foreign Affairs of the Spanish Republic, Alvarez del Vayo, in his book *Freedom's Battle*:

'It was the finest example of the art of handing victims over to the aggressor States, while preserving the perfect manners of a gentleman and at the same time giving the impression that peace is the one objective and consideration.'[1]

There is no more to be said.

1. J. Alvarez del Vayo, *Freedom's Battle*, London, 1940, p. 252.

Index